Intricate Emotion

Intricate Emotion

Downside of Discursiveness

Brian Moilanen

authorHOUSE®

AuthorHouse™
1663 Liberty Drive
Bloomington, IN 47403
www.authorhouse.com
Phone: 1-800-839-8640

First published by AuthorHouse   1/5/2010

ISBN: 978-1-4490-7144-8 (sc)

Printed in the United States of America
Bloomington, Indiana

This book is printed on acid-free paper.

ABOUT THE AUTHOR

Talk about a bizarre and unusual man, I bet you that Brian Moilanen is one that will hit the mark with both his life and with his writing. Brian Moilanen began his writing career as primarily a lyricist and singer for the rock band titled Guillotine, back in the year 1987, when Brian was a sophomore in high school. The band lasted for about 5 or 6 months before it met its demise due to know specific reason or logic. But during this time Moilanen managed to write about 6 fairly successful song lyrics ranging from fantasy to fiction to one song which was a graphic song all about nuclear war. This is how he got his writing start or beginning. And eventually dramatic results followed! He loosely played in bands for the next ten to twelve years and enjoyed himself a lot but had the same outcome of all of his rock bands. All these rocks bands seemed to be predestined to have short lives despite all of the raw talent. Moilanen claims his talent as a lyricist versus that of a singer was pretty equal. Moilanen's career on the other hand with poetry has been more short lived in time duration but he has won some major contests such as the Michigan State fair in 2007. He won first place for the poem titled "Flying without wings" and was against stiff and quite sophisticated competition as he acquired the literary writer of the year award. Brian is exceedingly proud of this accomplishment and plans to enter other contests down the road.

I hope this book is rewarding both for you and for me. May it be fulfilling with its thought and as a final result to say the least, bring a smile to your face and touch a soft spot within you. Enjoy!

A SUMMER'S DAY

Artistic skies canvas meticulously
regenerating heavens adorned above
Watch these ecclesiastical happenings
As assailing goes the billowing dove
The sun generously shines down
Beaming down invigorating vibrant heat
I relax and kick back in my gentle seat
No worries
I make friends with
My soothing inner voice
Contemplation noticeable and echoing
Reasons to rejoice
No hassles
Zero bothers
From this crazy world this is uttering and near
Understanding priceless love
And turning from detrimental fear
Simple joys are a
Necessity to get us by
Mischievous confused children
But hiding their ardor they continue to try
Passed love ones
Remain in my soul
Watching the grill burn with hamburgers
Amazed as my eyes catch the flaming coal
Walks through the trails
An abundantly warm sunshine is lighting the path
Detouring from evils of this land
Taking the time to understand God's wrath
Bible in hand
I decide to read some scripture
Beauty enlightens
And paints the most marvelous picture
My eyes shed a tear
No longer remaining dry
Tears with an erratic smile
Is my efficacious cry
Victory is today
A win that did do play
Realize that you can and will win
With even just prayer alone
Once you hear your calling
Do not prohibit yourself from
being near any spiritual phone
For this now is sincere and for real
Like a thief in the night
One time sin will be exercised by Christ
Yet that is at the worlds end
Until then
With worldly muse-he just won't bend

ANTIDOTAL ANSWER

This contagious disease
Being threatening and lethal
Has me immediately on bowed knees
Spiritual warfare is
Far from it's demise
Conflicts of character
How should we revise
Games that people play
Are sometimes cruel and abrupt
Still we carry on as civilian soldiers
In a game that is corrupt
Please give me some purity
In a world of distrust
Decaying minds are snit
And smothered in rust
Chaos and lies
Divert spoken honesty
Perjury or truth
Is there a chance for modesty
The Pied Piper
Was the enticer of leading utmost confusion
Waging wars
And beit portrayed as an illusion
It is hard to believe
What you can't see
Begging pleading people
Just want to be free
Hatred today has
Climbed to new heights
Such as a speeding roller coaster descending
Pushed into promiscuous plights
Plentitude is a rekindled desire
Much like a match with wood
The ability to make fire
Politics is shrewdness
With both managing and dealing
Now as high as the clouds
Yet what is the feeling
Antidotes and euphoria
Is this part of the cure
Analyzing myself blended within this world
I am not quite sure

ANTIQUE TOY SOLDIER

I am being held in stringent servitude
To your every single wish
Succeeding is pleasing you
I suppose the rules state this must I accomplish
Living life for others
My sole existence now
Takes a distant second place
Running madly into pandemonium
With all efforts to finish this race
Hostage holding
I am a prisoner too
And yes my mind is molding
Hope the future allows for someway of escape
Hung out to dry
Heavy laden burdens that do drape
My plate is spotless
Nothing at all to scrape
Uniquely an uncontrollable force
Is now my master
The storms eye is looming
If mankind's safety efforts are too yielding
The danger will lash and be consuming
Laws of logic apply
The plans that are made
Yet black listed and trapped in this hell
I search for the shade
Deadlines and orders
Essentials that equate
To what is mandatory
The pages being torn out
Difficulty in finishing this story
Indication allows only to improvise
The pawn hunting the oppositions noble king
A prognostication that possibly forecasts grand devise
Within the cards
There appears no treaty
Unapproachable differences
Gluttony equated with power can be so greedy
Can you not see that this war
Won't just end now
Slaughtering tanks are merciless
And onward they do plow
Mortar bombs fly
Incinerating all within it's path
Horror exemplifies the cry
And therefore is demised as cataclysmic wrath
A gap in time
Supreme distance in space
My memory unfocused yet allied amongst paradox
Was I actually at this place
De- ja-vu will supply clean truth such as clorox
My mind plays tricks
With my unfurling wallpaper like body
Yet a child's overwrought hands contort me

And put me now in dizzying motion
That is if I were to sell
Briefly please take the notion
This glass case I am enclosed within
Is that of a cell
From my mouth certain off color words do expel
I am the antique toy soldier that never did sell

ARE YOU HOLDING IT ALL IN?

Are you one of which that has befogged emotion that holds it in
Refined complex feelings diverged as both delicate and deep
And a reaction of despondency feels as if almost a sin
Hold it all in - yet if so as mentioned I will feel as if I am a creep
My mug of coffee appears as if boiling
And now on the carpet this brown steam overflowing begins to seep
Is there a connection there
And if there was- would I screw up this riddle or maybe even its care
With my bottled emotions
Should I let them all out
Could I please come to an assured solution
Anyway about it I will just likely gingerly pout
Who will see me if I decide to let them flea
Will any aggressors rage me if I become true
After what I consider is the real me
Will I lose my choice
Will I be cheated of my opportune chance
Even though I never really could
I would love to teach a holy angel on just how to dance
It might just be like a connected secular yet secure
Dream that is also absorbed with plenty of what appears as romance
So maybe I should just let myself go
Become like a baseball pitcher
And with fastball in hand begin to throw
I am the ultimate of confusion you could say
My emotions and feelings versus my brain and conscience
Are at war as they begin to play
I am dumbfounded
As I search for words to say
Befuddled
Maybe now such as before because I am at a loss
My heart beside me
With which I have not much choice yet too toss
I change my mind
Because I am the boss
I have come to a conclusion
I must free myself
I have no gifts to give myself
That which is elementary politics and I fashion of the Christmas elf
Is this a dilemma I am in or a glimpse at inner freeing
Just what is what
And what is it that I am truly seeing
I try not to beat myself up
Which is usually what I do
My foot is standard or normal
Yet large is the fit -you could call it the shoe

Are you my friend?

So much to lose
I suppose what is there truly to win
I hold the bubble containing virtue
And yet it is you who holds the distressing breaking pin
I attempt to hold contentment- grasping unto hope
Yet sometimes am wary and self realization enters into chagrin
You now as strange as it is
Become a stranger to a sort to your own patterns
Always needing light you gainfully go
Yes it is daytime therefore I don't see the sense of any lanterns
Is trust the key word or shortened phrase- what is this
basically all about
I have met more financially abundant than you
But they consider themselves not measured with sizable clout
Can time lend a hand
Or will time pick sides
For moments as this I see an over abundance of
Seconds and not minutes
And feel like I need a shove
Not from the assailing winds
Not form an iced earth
Not from a fires rekindling
Or even from my once supposed joyous birth
I need to realize
In some ways we think alike
We both know what it is to calmly live
And on the flip side
We obviously know what it is to see red with its infernal hate
Occasionally if we can understand these informalities
We can breathe air into lifeless lungs whispering its not too late
Ups and downs
Likewise downs and ups
Examine and speculate within your own soul first
To see what is potentially hazardous and just what corrupts
The first time I saw you
I need ed that feeling of genuine intrigue
Seeing forthright we were on the same team
And possibly batting in the same league
Do you know what I mean
Do you see what I say
Life is an on going inversion of tenacity with spontaneous theatrics
Yet much different than an arbitrated play
You have to find a true friend
One that gives maybe more than they take
If you are able to meet these credentials
We have made a connection for heaven sake
I miss you from time to time
Even when you are ever so close
My supposed medicine is calling
But thought of you quickly remedies as that of an antidotal dose
Thoughts equal as if to emotionally feel
Feelings anchor my emotions
And actions put my concentrations of mind into rewind
Because the y have taught
Yet there is still much more in the two of us to find

BLACK SHEEP HAND

It is quite clever
The crooked contriving
Of a preplanned life
Free wills limitations
Orthodox hopes becoming overshadowed in strife
Don't know until you try
Effervescence dies
When I am no longer high
Euphonic sounds no
Longer to be heard
Direction now must be made
To keep me from the absurd
Suspicious of what
The maker does make
Sadly so the unqualified
Shall eventually burn in the fiery lake
Black sheep hand
Shoved out of this organization
Pushed out of this earth
What is the meaning
Of my once joyous birth
I push rigorously to succeed
Yet there is a dagger thru heart
Watch as I bleed
My mouth becomes lemony tart
This faltering hand
Makes living twice as hard
Trust just
A few
That you bring
Into your life
Reconcile with attainable diverse forgiveness
And drop the knife
An unpleasant war
In my head
Is what this pensive soldier has said
I see it in the middle
But play it straight
So much is predictable
Playing cards intervened heavily with fate
The fortunate dine
In banquet form
Residing in luxury
And pointing fingers what is different that they see
Establishment of forgiveness
The teaching of goodness and diversity
I believe that this is
Still within reach
If not my remote efforts are just
Too distant as I try and preach

BLACK SHEEP HAND PART 2

Tragic as it may eventually drastically seem
We are now more spiritually and environmentally close
Four shots of vodka is my receptive cure
And as I see it -it is my required dose
Almost feeling content although my face where's only a sigh
Charming
Almost harming
Repentance and forgiveness if misunderstood and not attributed
Is graven and quite alarming
Limiting your perfection
Yet the flipside is a form of deliverance
Take these words as you may
Some call this sustenance of verbal eloquence
Tragedy
Some live to speak of their debacle
Fate tests us I believe
Not the other way around
The cards played you probably
If the once was you -is now six feet underground
All the pain that was once inflicted
Took it's unprecedented demise too early
The towns conversations about now have become conflicted
Babe in the woods
My love so precious gone earthly for apparently all time
Such as prehistoric dinosaurs demise seen no more
Le Brea tar pits my feet scathed within slime
My heart touches base from bottom up in solace
The conglomeration of emotion with balanced instinct
And uncanny intelligence puts you the teacher at the podium
A salty white substance occurring essential to the body's
Fluid balance we concur this and with that as sodium
For all tragedies end don't they
In this I have learned money is of focus and essential to obtain
Yet I have been unfairly stripped of
So how may I pay
Unfortunately in true grim regard
The biosphere was set before life began
Chromosome and D.N.A inclinations to regard nonfunctional
All this sadly was part although of the sick plan
The heartaches on this individual are habitual
My wants are merely your needs
Evading nightmares and hopes of chasing dreams become ritual
Fortify although these strange times subsequently
Seeing what and who gets left is residual
And became the targets of cheap shots of authority frequently
Get right with God
Words perpetuated by both my friend and enemy alike
A hundred plus turn against company tyrants to instigate
The altercation of holding a major strike
For I doubt he is paid with just enough to accomplish only his needs
And his main transportation becomes his bike
Much pondering doubt
Piece of mind
Equation of thought

More than half of my lives battles
Were unnecessary and need not staged or fought
That is if you know what I mean
Where am I at within thoughts and transitions
I have successfully completed the change
Yet financial success within all the ongoing headaches
Life just seems so overwhelmingly real
Maybe although you could do me a favor
And pass on the good word for the day being zeal
For those written out may they be written in
I am collecting change in my cup
For worldly change and it is desperate and made of tin

BRAIN WASHING

My satisfaction begins to plunder and not grow at all
Inundating my brain although educated within turmoil I feel the strain
And wonder if paranoia is real and I am set to take a fall
Heroism
Will I be able to self exalt as to this a claim
For I have never been a follower
And as one predominantly just the same
Sometimes I carousingly lead
And sometimes I will blindly follow
Ironically I believe I am not of this worldly contemptuousness
A rusted saint I am more of being naked yet hallow
Barbituates
Yes they almost do stupefy as helping to induce sleep
Habituates
A soul engaged into sin changes in the shadows such as sheep
What should I do when in these transition purifying modifications
Translations
Expirations
At the expiration laughing or in lamentations
Renditions
Expeditions
A way from myself in this fragile mental state
Make an effort not to hate
Just wait
Time heals wounds medically so
Don't let the critical inner voice become far too irate
Brain storming
Practicality of just conforming in a mental way
Hearing now of these triumphant dreams while revealing plans
Brain washing
Make evidently clear your work is absolute and very pure
As I am put through these agonizing mental correction scans
Your peace pipe holds its way to validity of circumstance
The green substance within allows benediction of soul with procedures
While the lessons within physically allow supernaturally even the dead to dance
Saints and sinners once saved- in heaven now have an eternal home
Yet are the numbers predetermined as these hierarchies freely roam
The sheep's here are vast and numerous wherever I am
And all of these numbered I must as in celebration comb
It is a dream in this cathartic state of mind
So much to seek
Obviously put henceforth so much to find
But back to earth I have often been lied about
Yes people have accused, cussed, and cheated me
Out of a life as it stands of sufficient worth
But I know I can't give up
I just can't give in
Friends of credentials with positive assertion
Don't you know
There is just so much to see
My Unadulterated ego seeks the alter ego to find it's place
And contentment whispers mimicking words that transpire as glee
Just which side is which
What truly represents what is up

When often times upside amounts to the side that is down
And you find yourself lost even more calloused within confusion
As you will even pay a large sum just to purchase a grin
Yet these dark nights lead eventually to sunlit filled days
I believe this so much
That somehow I know certainly there is an angel in waiting
And slow anticipation finds this elusive magical touch
In this game of life
My thoughts I hope are still mine
Although you may read into them as if reading an open book
Maybe I am reading your game of life book
Intrigue follows intensely as I take a look
And latch on secondarily with a fishing hook

BRILLIANCE OF LIGHT

A longed craving to see
The light at the distant tunnels end
Structures of science completely prudent
To God allowing for all to comprehend
Morning, day, and night
Possibly instinctually not sure of motive or force
Welcome now to this luminous possibly ordained light
Hierarchical beings possibly inspire this fulfilling source
Call this if you will a higher power
In a world where we sometimes don't feel free
And carry on although watched from the wretched guard tower
Right now you can let down your continued guard
And let your inhibitions continue to run on high
Because seeing and securing this inner freedom
Silences the oppressor creating for them something to deny
A breath of fresh air
Clean air in the lungs
No longer sabotaged with being fraudulently distraught
Evil vile spewed from the forked tongues
What was prayed for was learned while being taught
Drastic changes must be made
And within this momentary euphoria I see it is just so
For love of my higher powers kingdom has much to seek
And with faith guiding my salvation I hope to someday go
Yes the dark feeds the shadows
Which allows pristinely for light from a cracked sky
Because full and complete Is now the desperate wailer
And no longer lonely finds the tear from your cry
I have seen your pain
And nearly ostracized I now am beside myself
Your not alone dear one
So unabashedly throw away burdens stacked upon the shelf
All of this trueness of reality accumulate within the plan
Seven angels
Seven separate stories of seven desperate souls
Other unique type prodigies
Not commanding yet instructing just what extols
It's such a high to currently be outside of this territory of space
My mind drawing nearer to forgetfulness
And painful memories an altruistic force seems to erase
The world on earth is running sad to say
Change their scrutinized hearts so they may keep the pace
And astonish with changed truth to silence foes uttering total dismay
I pray in virtue that this heaven is always near
For it drives away all viable evils
And keeps my mind, body, and soul in the clear
Vacated from hurt
Erased from all wars both artificial and real
Onward in steadfastness I must exert
This unique moment allows me to evermore feel

CALMING THE COMBAT

Controversies
Lies, corruption and such
Chaos is intact and breeding
Welcome to devilish touch
Emotions and articulate words that are honest
Seem to divide
A plane departs with fuel mistakenly deplete
Yet very quickly flawed it begins to glide
An evil work is nearly complete
Behind the scenes
Where did this tragic error begin
Wandering minds diverge
And become confused scathing with sin
Or was this an error at all
Somewhere malice will
Fall to discord and be potently perverse
Somewhere someone shakes hands
With these devils
Seven heavens attribute although with the
Angry angels avenging from all levels
Because this substance of poison
Does have catalyst of remedy
A war in these worlds
Opens the eyes for even the blind to see
Jubilation utmost and frolics itself
Within this fun filled excitement spree
Mankind is diverging
In this critical situation
Just how much sin comprised evil
Does God allow in his most glorious creation
Appropriation of war
Is it though on the same field and elevation
Operations of good versus evil
Strengthened families
Harmoniously stay strong as the core
Prayers to the Almighty
Derived from a thousand nuns
Fulminate skies portray
The Angry angels canvassed above
Devils resembling teradactyles
Contending with eagles yet fearing the dove
Black magic and witchcraft
Slanders within it's own kind
The President will universally end this war
Just in case I need to remind
Not a solitary event
Please convert the naysayer
Options wisely promote to repent
And to obtain admittance with simplicity of prayer
Because those cast in hell
Without doubt will see it is too late
Concurring too much with what is wrong
And bringing discerned biographies about their prevalent hate

CAN YOU CONCEAL THE MADNESS

Is appears as if a raging quandary
Just what should I do with this circumstance
The pit bull menacingly looks on and seems as if it will attack
Should I run
Should I pose threat to save my ass
This predatory animal knows no bounds
And as my senses are dulled I must definitely still pass
If I fail
I will get hurt and possibly fall victim to death
My heart is pumping quite hard
And I cannot even hear my own panicked voice let alone my own breath
I have walked this road before
And this time the last
Yet I have made up my mind
Everything from before was cheerful yet that was the past
How time can change
Although the stimuli remains unchanged
I think that my mind unfortunately has let vertigo in again such as before
A ghost seeps within the door
And is restless and cold and he needs to explore
Now my mind is fixated on two worries
A haunted car door and a menacing dog
If I don't react
I could become a bacon meal such as fried hog
I begin to run
And run hard at that
The dog eyes me up and he dashes after me as I am his last meal
My mind is perplexed and horrified
Shit…I'm not toast along with flavor cooked veal
I look back
I now hear a car horn as my heart thumps through my shattered soul
I feel as a cheated innocent fugitive who is running on parole
The car horn screams
As the dog catches my leg
I don't know as how to fight this off but through hate and fire
I will not go down
I will not become part of this evil empire
I kick the dog in the biting face
It jostles off whelping in utter pain
My life continues
Now this was a true gain
The car door although opens and closes
Closes and opens
Repetition again and again
So damn much it almost seems like sin
Those damn devils behind it
Are surfacing and I know I must act again to win
A dark prophet I am yet a prophet still indeed
How about you do the gathering and you finish this story
But that is not how this does end
I decide to run
And run an run an run is what I did do
I ran for seventeen miles all the way to town

Just to find
myself finding morning and a way through
I feel tired- yet hindsight
As it can be a weapon of honest attack- finds me as new

CHAIN OF COMMANDS

Allegations
Simply put
Can be the grace of arbitrations
Is the statue of liberty singing
Opinion offers itself with what to decide upon
Are you near enough to hear freedoms bells ringing
Strangely enough though with division
Fingers to point
Colleagues do blame
Understanding in this business world
We do not all operate the same
Barraged with questions
Character flaws will disclose
Finding honest people
Without hidden agendas to expose
Gaining combinations to
Sincere and loyal people
Take the wintertime fun
To put the wreath on the church steeple
What links common folks
Groups and generations
Identifications in life
Offered from most if not all situations
Low keyed rebellion
Falls out of the sorts
To high keyed power
A small fortress yet with mighty strength
To succeed you must climb that tower
Do not oppress or prejudgingly bring down
If so character defamation and calumny
Falsely labels you as the clown
Which as you know must be avoided at all cost
Such as breathing in air from a semi
Almost inexcusable is the exhaust
Yet so goes the aggravation
Do I make myself clear
Or is it me unsure and full of procrastination
Never lose sight
Of duty or obligation
A congenial communion
Yielding itself as a annotation of association
Attentive to communal and
Analytical and authoritative views
Allow for your life to be a victorious story
Shining brightness and allows focusing with good news

CHARTING NEW WATERS

Shot heard cross the world
Gymnastic efforts
Handstands with flips acrobatic while having twirled
Beneficial collaboration
Wholehearted dealing with the need to succeed
Yet there is a cut
And a desire to stop the bleed
Can't make up my mind
From time to time
What's the verse
And henceforth what about the rhyme
But one thing drive me insane
Sometimes just one thing
Completely makes me tick
Unprecedented concerns
Eliminate from this engrossed clique
Yet why is this so
Mind modification is the entailed pitch
That the clever baseball pitcher does throw
And now this ball player is on my team
He establishes my concentrated efforts
And demonstrates the availability of living a dream
A dream
A wish
Everything worth the efforts of achieving
Or what I say Is to accomplish
Play life hard
Not meager and weak
You have to adjust your game
Until everything does tweak
Nobody said or claims victory is easy
Do it for others also
Until they are tired of saying please me
Loved ones
When they are near the bodies feelings are deep and far
As the astrological moon filled night's
Accompanied by you that one star
Nice to have seen you
The memory I hold dearly within
Naughty angels compromise
Righteousness with sin
Uncharted paths
The boat side waters
Causing the plummet
Yet climbing the mountain
And surfacing at the top of the summit
Exploring new worlds
Differentiating between
What is wrong and right
Be careful as the winds are shifting
And frantic flies the kite

COLLECTIVE IMAGINATION

Just exactly what is it
That reoccurs and goes amongst this chronic brain
Seemingly habitual
The principles equate to the definition apparently as refrain
Something supernatural a unique and amazing force
Guidance directed and completely displayed this day
A byproduct of an untouchable Godlike source
Inner workings of the mind
Are interestingly supple and easy to bend
A life supposedly long seems short if happy and successful
And to this understanding beit I must attend
What happens just by chance
Sometimes lures itself utterly and in direct portion
Be quick not to be allured by what is vile and evil
Or other similar deceptions call it extortion
Collective thoughts
Sometimes appear as large colossal views
Do your homework with it's tests
And push rigorously negotiating the reviews
A benediction
May this comfort your favour and elegant favor
A feast such as toasting to kings and queens
With the taste succulent and much to savor
Pacify
Reply
Don't deny
Good future endeavors now will comply
Can you read my mind
Will I by chance read yours
Onward the battle continues
And as though charging this military travels the shores
Use your brain, soul, conscience, and mind
Obviously what once becomes popular and trendy
Always returns again in the form of rewind
Even if not government issued
And as an accredited soldier as claim
Pursue your dream
And win this battle just the same
Tarnished thought
Collective soul
A war once fought
Even with flat tires shall continue to roll
Commonalty
Everyday average Americans are stars
We help form United States of fifty
And starlight overshadows along with small mighty planet Mars
Let your brain run rampant
Maybe your body will again unite
This well wound mechanical being
Can not forsake or give up this inspirited fight
Do not file a grievance
If I am not overtly or graciously not too polite

CONFLICT OF CONSPIRACY

When and if corruptibly conspired against
I definitely will doggedly fire back with my military cannon
Now being armed with colossal massive mental aggression
My mouth not shut beit that this now is my confession
For I will not tolerate this attempt at organized oppression
I am now seeking only enough to avoid this act of suppression
While allocating only to utmost despair and nerving depression
I tally up these figures equaling to an evil spirited tension
Which is or acts as a mental outpost of daily activity of complete suspension
Guard the parameter
Make sure to efficiently get the job done
These bastards will lose
And I will turn the tables finding them who are now on the run
I have run
You made me do the job of having to hide one time too much
Acidic rain
It has pelted my body and is not a warming soft touch
You see what I say
Do you know what I mean
At any rate
Is this war that I am beleaguered within
All testimonial truth of a twist of fate
If I am not comprehending or am now currently at a loss for words
Does this ascribe to detrimental hate
Maybe I should have the best offense
That is undermined by an extravagant defense
Do I make sense
Or is my ultimate game plan now becoming perplexed
Hexed
Fill in the blanks and let God write your text
Is this true
Wow.....this is so real
Because now with this situation of titular cataclysm
We I believe shall all see
The end of this war and a demise is a fantastical dream
These idiotic ones shall pay for their ambushed attack
And their necks I shall outwardly ream
Sometimes war is needed when peace has no chance to stand
It is absolution for the troops and their families
You could call it detrimental demand that unfortunately gets retrenched through combat
Listen up to the word
And do not act as a brat
Fighting
Killing
War at All ends
This one we will claim as being the victor
And not play it in as charades
Get er' done
Or do not even try
If you are not on my team
Then shut up because I don't want to hear if you with smite r

CONFUSION ILLUSION

Absurd; Ridiculous
Nearsightedness finally understands this glory
Idiocy finds itself nestled within this fortress
And within everybody's own illustrated quixotic story
Pictures in the mind connect with what is transverse
Yet these are practical measures of our actions
And habitual walls comfort as I rehearse
The relationship within yet not without my soul and spirit
Allows for these tender lips to regale themselves
Feeding the god's my discussion while consequently filled with grace
Crazy decisions in the past sometimes turned out right
Beside the anchorage of sin within this human race
Restless tension this earthly relationship is uniquely discourse
A teeter tauter battle of good vs. evil
I say invaluable because mind war does instigate force
Is this a mass illusion
A complete mind confusion
Shall we say a twisting of the brain
Not sure of these camouflaged faces as friend or foe
Ardently your efforts are worthy although they must indeed keep you sane
Writings on the wall equate to principles that add up
Where I can read it complete yet very plain
Is my dread only understood by restless souls
A fable or relentless parable
Let us pray that earthly remedy extols
Transmute
Change my life into something that indeed has condition
Refute
I gather and compute to deny those claims in my expedition
Dispute
Seemingly always a byproduct of any contradiction
Pollute
Be careful because the air we breathe can cause infliction
Translate
It is easier done than said
Perpetuate
Don't be a statistic as the dead
Change gears
Do not fall victim and as prey in a carnal land
A high decibels voice used with vocals take action
Refreshingly has its authoritative command
Defy logic and measures of modern science
Beating the odds
The apex of being connected to an alliance
Branded
Stranded
A surreal glimmering light at tunnels end
While through it all clinging to faith
While society's aim is to apprehend
Armed with instruction's needle and thread
Repairing past injustices while beginning to mend
Just what is your magical charm
Bestowed by maybe delusion or fantasy
Allowing until for now nothing to attack or blatantly harm

CONTINUED GAMES

Now I believe the
Games are over
In actuality
They really have just begun
Negotiating with crawl and walk
I decide to run
Pain with pleasure
The shovels dig
Despite findings of any treasure
Now there is a darkening grey area in between
Yet sometimes the grey area
Is all that I see
A ballistic emotional rage
Occasionally begins with a tainted mind
A lifetime of obligations
A slave to the grind
Hold back the rage
And hope contentment will
Embody with blessing
Count your blessings now
To reduce the stressing
Hate doesn't motivate
It is a destroyer of serenity and soul
Spiraling downward vertigo
Ultimate confusion of place and mind
Conclusions of I just don't know
What does tomorrow bring
What have the yesterdays taught
The gloves are weathered
Because in that ring I too have fought
Pacify using harmonious
Words to lavishly calm
Christian literature
Beautiful music creates this psalm
Love conquers all
Prior to the bitter end
Contemplations of right and wrong
Just what initiates our insidious sin
Joy is entwined with
A thick barbed prickly vine
Zero limitations
Infinite qualities create what is divine
The time is now
Turn a cheek
Humanitarian efforts
The agnostic does seek
Contrarily though
Christian ways also subsequent
This estranged soul
Paying with beliefs and actions
Yet there is no financial toll
Existing is an answer
Blessing hearts with our meditative thoughts

CONVERSATION PIECE

I try to comprehend
Infinity forever
Heaven or hell
Dwelling places to abode
With infinite stories to tell
Torture and torment
Or loving peace and joy
Dying old man
Or infant with toy
What is the criteria to enable this employ
Once a human life to this earth is conceived
A soul shall be permanent or say always existent
And this being more than just what is commonly perceived
An infidels ego and also their logic seem to deflate
Birth, live, die, and grave
There is more too expect as I begin too feel irate
I too have spoken to many type agnostic minds
Yet ratio integrity with much more than just hate
Nearly impossible to perceive
A soul that has passed either is descended or ascended
Now there is no charity that allows you to leave
Where do you draw the line
Does a line need to be drawn at all
For the record
Apostle Paul's original name was Saul
Angels, saints, and spirits
These are all inspirations from God
Guarding and protecting
Wings flying
They are able to resurrect
They bring to life
Both miracles and a surplus of love
Holy beings
That fly like a dove
Do not allow for cynicism to drag you
Or push false pretenses into your brain and all about
Even though poor and meek
You my friend have demonstrated colossal clout
Who cares you say
Others say you must
For faith in mankind in itself will fall apart
And from within the structure will rust
Is forever here
Is forever there
Is infinity going to be everywhere
In reverence to clairvoyance
These are my understandings which I needed to share

DEAR GOD

God
In the tomorrow
God
In the today
Illuminating angels
Divinely focused demonstrating the Savior's promised way
Inspired and affined
By the master
These celestial being encompass
And protect from any unfortunate coming disaster
Examine your past
Certain beautified moments
Never perish consequently they only last
Within the brain
Inside the mind
Nostalgia plays it's roll
What was fond now returns in the form of rewind
Euphoria creates
Euphoria demonstrates
Ultimate fulfillment of all senses unique
Distant uttered words
Yet nobody found to speak
Have you spoken to God today
With infinite pure and genuine desire
Anonymously today a new soldier has been employed
With all the trials and tribulations God did still hire
Am I ready for the test
This test being time
Whistling harmony and hymn create my music
Ultimately this creates sanctimony with rhyme
Beckoning are the tones and songs
From the heavens
Our Savior's righteously graced spiritual numbers
Are most often seen as sevens
Seven angels
Seven miracles
Seven continents that form
This territory that it's earthly inhibitors dwell
Unrelenting
Repenting
Entwined within a benevolent spell
Even if your eyes were deviously shut
Or you were once blind
Forgiveness of past transgressions
Blotted out sins that the Maker has just signed
See the light
Light of ordained brilliance
One that always shines
Without end omnipotent is the resilience
Hope
Pray
Without shield or sword avenge for
Enemies to retreat reclusively into dismay

DECEPTIONS AND LIES

It all comes out in the wash
Subtleness of time passing pervades altruistically
Secrets to be revealed
The crowd of chosen followers runs blind temporarily
But with this truth obtainable their fate is sealed
Deceptions
Receptions
What lies beneath
So compelling it steals your concluding thought
As an angry voice mutters behind the teeth
Suspicion lies at the doorsteps unknowingly while
Grim hope shows your utter resignation
Partnerships that prove far from loyal
Wondering who is who
And caught seemingly endless within the vast turmoil
Armed with compass and map yet strangely without direction
Now thereafter just what to do
I smell a rat surfacing the odor not the only detection
Within what secrets does honesty contain
Living this life of dirty laundry exposed
Yet some say still say my belief is all in vain
Dejection
Correction
May you hear and speak only truth of me
This aversion allows only for bad memories to remain intact
Yet divine nature return with soundness the ability to flea
You reneged on your offer to keep this unsaid
I shall retract back to my world with feelings not yet settled
I attempt to put aside shame as I walk amongst the dread
No vengeance within me no not as of yet
Yet I revamp upon all of this guess work
And I am not sure with it just what I will get
A second chance
When my first chance should have not been dismissed
.The game of mental calculations with strategy utmost
I see certain qualities omitted from this moderate list
When a deception is thrown
Darkness of lies tarnishes
Allowing that vindicator to cast from his corrupt throne
Just what is left to do
What is the retaliation
Sneaking in seeds of salvation
Upon the cultivated plantation
Because I also have deceived and lied and such
A 50-50 dinner treat if you will
Pleasing to see the return of the favor same as the dutch
My past doggedness carouses the opportunity to forgive
Foundations of what I call true values
So that we all may coexist and onwardly live
Business can be bloody in the figurative
Yet still unique and illustrious form
Stay away from what is hidden vile and corrupt
Although you see this as a mainstream norm
Create your own rules broken one so you do not forcibly erupt

DEFINING CONTENTMENT

Problems always exist
Like planets that revolve
Past vital amends given
Yet just exactly what did they resolve
Understand where I stand
I am a soldier with batteries charged to full tilt
Unlike a dying flower
I am sure that as of today I will not wilt
I follow the ultimate command
Because when making these galaxies
God put much effort and demand
Time through the hourglass
And filled abundantly with sand
Mystery is the story
That the infant does define
Love does blossom
Can't you see the obvious sign
Time is the essence
Of a slow anticipation
With spiritual intervention inhibited
Witnessing our own creation
Innocent to the world
A strange generation awaits
Actions, deeds and beliefs
Constitute heavens opens gates
The fractured mirror
Lies on the ground
Impact evident
My life now I suspect I have found
The pieces come together
No longer being lost
Having ample money
Yet seeing no cost
Joy shines and plays it's part
An orange luminous body
The astronomical sun is now my heart
Mild joy shakes hands
With harmony
Scholarly minds
Just might fabricate and confidently agree
Put on the denims
Slide on the T
Off again I go
Moving as a canoe
Strength propels against the undertow
Happiness is your goal
And you play the lead role
Give this soul a dream
And inclinations of hope
Because I am climbing higher
And won't lose grasp of the rope

Depleted Status Only Lasts Temporarily

Depleted
Yet without indication or doubt
Avenging forward I always have competed
Let this world know what you are about
Understand where I come from
And the words in which I speak
Wise yet young so do not allow for untrue deprivation
Because I will get a lawyer if you label as a geek
Where I would be without proper height for elevation
Hit the target
Make your mark
If done in cordial respect
Shame on the critics who blemish with cruel remark
Get quality accredited education
Beit formal or informal
Because evidently it is an instrument of supplication
It will provide you with what you really need
Maybe even become a profusion of what is undeniable good
If you like what you see granted continue to read
Which not allowing for depression confidently I do understand
Love, joy and other high tidings equate to my prediction
Do your what appears as your endless now
And work with and not against yourself allocating void of all restriction
Love your neighbor while not forgetting yourself
Stock up on all those good times with picture perfect memories
And bank them good as gold upon the family picture shelf
Do not keep from using or enjoying my formula of description
Because If I do not find a job soon
I could be at a loss and facing eviction
Will I make a million
Or even to a ballistic minimum a common buck
The thunder and lightning in the colored skies
If I am not entrusted with faith I might get painfully struck
What is your environment like
Are you at peace for even your own sake
Count your blessings and prerogatives at laud
And thank your higher power each time that you awake
Or to be more precise let us refer to him as God
Have not seen you in years
Tracing my mind in thought it seems it has been eons
Sentimental afflictions evident as I hold back the pressing tears
Who am I
What have I become
Melancholy is rattling my cage of present self absorption
Sadness secondary and first place claims the stage being glum
Yet this depleted status lasts only temporarily
Reading sacred text along with it's passages
Everything curtails to testament of prophecy beginning as verily
Never stop believing in yourself today, never or ever
Manifestation of promises reciprocate nearly always expendable worth
If ever in tribulations rely on angels deemed as clever
For now we shall depart yet again we will meet
I greatly appreciate your generous fulfilling heart
And at our church for two I am obliged that you saved me a seat

DESPITE ALL MY SINS

Touching hearts
When there was not need for any touch
These deceitful words revile
And complicate fact exceedingly much
Terminated at point of contact
Helplessness is the focus of target
Of the oppositions attack
Strongly firing back with mental ammunition
This lone wolf transcends without the pack
Condition of a wicked brain
Commences itself foreseeing no compromise
Seeing the self as the only one with worth
A hallow head
Measures uneducated and with zero girth
Uninformed in decisions
A stubborn mind is unyielding
And on course to be void of vital divisions
Baptized shortly after birth
Understanding that we are all born into sin
My brain injured intensely accepts this humiliation
A key ingredient of this vexatious chagrin
The same as any
I have hurt
And have been hurt
We have all resembled cobras
As ancient ancestors have slithered in dirt
Yet sanctimony sets dominoes into collide
Good versus evil
It is time to choose your side
In the end
I have confidence you will let me in
I too have chosen
And recourse with my defective sin
Spiritual warfare
Is a living empathy to mankind
More than three mice running
And no we are not blind
I see the balance of life as revealed overture
The hands of time are always moving forward
Faith has it's magic and daily it is assured
If your glasses are dirty
Open your eyes wide and your vision won't be blurred
Day dreaming is a remedy
While witness the pain it has relieved
Time passes quickly
And just cannot be retrieved
Despite the sweetness
It's actions are not easily achieved
All my knowledge
I lay on the table
This great enchantment embodies me
And is as enticing as a fable
My condition is content
These shed tears prove it is not too late

With attainment being focused I learn to repent
Despite my failure
May God see me though it all
As if walking on tight ropes
Thanks for carrying me so not to fall

DIRECTIONS THROUGH DELUSION

Osmosis
Psychosis
One equates to the processes of chemical diffusion
Uniquely enough though these do not appear to combined
As if betrayal of truth or merely enchanted illusion
Are all men created equal
Or do the cards just land where they may
Obligations to keep you posted and informed of a stony sequel
Heart, soul, body and mind
Practicality measures itself in full regard
The clock in forward motion abstained from rewind
Open to legitimate forms of pursuit
Sadly enough this situation concludes with its disparages
And other qualities that could grimly pollute
Games
Claims
Are you near enough to hear what this story exclaims
Do not turn your back for too long
Because obviously impact is evident
And forthright the point that we plead is strong
Lives road is long and always full of
Unexpected fateful bends and predisposed twists
Just as if militant soldiers and through the bizarre we march
As our conscious confusions resists
Just what goes wrong in the brain
Maybe in our ginger hearts causes something to go right
Because a well wound soldier is not able to abandon the fight
Preening
Do not become engrossed with importance and self worth
Nostalgia
At any rate remember every ending causes another's birth
What do you assert to be a quality of value
Gimmicks
Trickery
Yet this is just a token of temporary light
Remembering the war is here and the heavens welcome
Those deemed fit open armed with significance of delight
Predictions
Restrictions
Whose to tell a transformable soul who's right or wrong
You have to keep yourself together
Battling along swiftly as if playing ping pong
Telepathy
Crystal ball
Untold future
Or maybe natures call
Some will climb
Others fall
Grown up now in total correspondence
Never again shall I crawl

Dirty slate

Is the slate now clean
Or is this merely a closed book
Not quite sure of just what is fact or fiction
Systems fail within my mind while vertigo manages to set in
Arms crossed poignantly I do greet this contradiction
Unknowingly the assemblage gawks and looks not authorizing a mental win
These blood shot eyes locate a vertical horizon
Yet off by a fraction therefore the view is slanted
Take these words in actuality not as a pun
Everything dramatically tipped from side to side
Assailing frantically goes this tilt-a-whirl
The ride uncomforting nestled between slide and glide
This amusement park ride without any foreseeable end
And so the story does go-what an unsettling ride
Inner collapsing my senses without justification to lend
Within the last hour alone I have had my 12th cup of joe
Why do you find pleasure in others pain
Like tide's shifting tables can quickly turn
While enemies without protection still run from the acid rain
Caught within a vacuum lost between time and space
Seemingly also void of light and dark too
That is this vacuum
May I also add without a loved one near
Hostage to fortune around the corner what just does loom
How can I run
When obviously there is no where to go
Being void of joy creates mental disharmony
Myself and money legitimate without fraud
Yet I do not know why you see me as phony
Where do we go when time seems to stand still
And in gross abundance lives do falter and fail
Limited understandings by most of those vexed
It can be like complete innocence yet stuck in jail
Am I blessed
Am I cursed
Even through mythology
Those in trying situations still blatantly rehearsed
Am I now the hiatus to my own situation
My illness of frustration quite trivial yet unique
I am growing tired despite a full night of sleep
Impact evident as I search for words just to speak
To let go of heartaches and frustrations
Likewise the main component is you
A level playing field you say will never happen
But on this field it is a one size all fits shoe
Make the change
Do not derange
And hope the cards land in all the best positions
Because many say the best way to succeed
Is to get away from these current mental inflictions

DO NOT RESENT PAST LOVE'S

Do not allow for illusion to incessantly cause mental malfunctioning fraud
Pay accordingly to past reference of joys
And externalize them in praise-or shall we say as in laud
The use of knowledge allows us to grow
Yet if not used properly carouses that optimizing that information blindly
Which allows for the adverse ultimatum of miniscule expectation to grow
Take some time to see where you stand
Being past emotions in the mind through memory alone become
Immortalized and have wisdom to show at heed and henceforth should vibrantly glow
Remember if possible only the good times
The laughter, the joy, the brilliancy of inner peace
Because within us all is a silent ticking time bomb
But a pacifist has the ability to safely release
Tranquility of heart; peace of mind
Look far behind within your personal nostalgic book
And you are bound to find
Love that was supposed to last forever
Promises were broken and defiantly cleansed in the tub
I am sinking beneath and below this informality of brokenness
And I am stuck in the murky waters of steel blue within my mechanized sub
I will not allow myself to be treated as less than human
Or so to say dirt underneath your scathing feet
Uncross your arms and open them up in a fellowship of love
As I desire open arms to readily greet
But that is all in the past
This is the terrific new today
Union of believers and also deceivers
Who form a pact or henceforth fellowship a brand new way
For love can definitely be real
Without it
Mankind and it creatures would be extinct
Because nature itself studies mankind
And through subtlety we are all linked
What is happening to joy, peace and for that matter
The simplicity of a random act of kindness
You think these words I say sound absurd
But without acting upon they measure and you would definitely miss
It is hard to get over a loved one or for that matter a lover
We are all equal
And therefore symbolically never was I above her
Take these words
Bank them
Embellish them
Listen to them in granted heed
They will embark you on the right path
Acknowledging you for the money yet separating you from the greed
I wish you luck on getting over your broken heart
But please remember this
Another love will arrive again
With oxygen, blood for the veins, and sympathy for the soul
This will keep lives game playing
And onward your spiritual battle of fun will continue to roll

DON'T JUDGE ME

Don't judge this book
By it's possibly unimpressive cover
Misunderstood interpersonal ways
Yet incognito plays
Actually a seducing lover
A soul here
Dies to be read
You are the reader
And therefore you hold the thread
Misconception of time
And acknowledgement of place
A legitimate alibi
Frees the accused truth without trace
Understand the issue
Before the accusations are thrown
The music plays
In it's subtle soothing tone
Together we create chemistry
That similar of being valid cure
Don't close your eyes
For the days just might blur
Smell the coffee brewing
Take action
And kick that depression to the curb
Unknowingly your position
Changes from noun to verb
Antidotes, medicines, and cures
All change from person to person
And henceforth from place to place
I am driving madly yet do not understand
Meaning of this wretched chase
Born exclusively into trouble
Yet educated quickly with change
My brain is perplexed
And quickly could derange
All minds are subjected
Circumstance relative of being subjected
To being torn into two
Angel on my shoulder
Demon on my back
Where did I go wrong
And just what do I lack
Attempting to place a finger only upon myself
You labeled me incorrectly
And my attempts become disarmed
These efforts sadly have failed
Your loving heart I have harmed
Forgive me
If you so choose
Not being that child
Whose stuck in those terrible two's

DOUBLE JEOPARDY TEMPTATION

Unthinkably tricky
A strange temptation
Amatory gives way to mental perspiration
Enticing words are added
That sink with lost souls
If so many know
Then who will take the bait
Predestined lessons allows conviction
Of morals at any rate
Brave new world
Our minds weigh
Both sides of tipped scale
Crash course in ethics
Yet I believe the train won't derail
We all have some skeletons in our closet
Some more than
Just a few
Yet they play it straight
The curious
Just usually don't have a clue
Others have different views
Claiming to drown
The obscure secret desire
The water drenches
And through time
Extinguishes the fire
Yet some live with childlike antics
And meddle with
What I prefer to call the unexplored
Temptation of this nature
So ultimately though
We question this questionable pleasure
And does or does not guilt give way
To any conceivable treasure
I really don't know
Only been there twice
As I was nearly consoled with riches and turned away
Construed with her words as my friend
Kept repeating what she had too say
A human disease that plagues us
Just like cancer
I myself prefer watching that one female dancer
Who wins over my heart
As she is a perfect rhythmic romancer
Don't ever forget the games attached
Innocence forsaken
And away it becomes snatched
Where and who
Do we turn
When playing with turmoil
Yet heartfelt desire to learn
Lost you say
For the moment

Within the today
Rationalizing with the gods
While abiding the Almighty
So He might hear what you say

DRUG

Not all of this madness was prescribed
Inspirations from these high times
I'm glad that I subscribed
This mortal life needs affection
With a satisfactory drug to feel alive
Trapped in this death defying combat
I long to survive
Do not deprive this necessity
Now I have the hunger too succeed
Lives pages
Continue to read
Likewise continue to write
Euphoric intervention
What is audible and what is within sight
Ask yourself this question
If life is short
Why not play it hard
Overcoming stipulations
Grass to grow the yard
There is a time and place
For everything
Now I need a place
For this time
The hill is steep
And relentless the climb
The only sounds I now hear
Are from conscience
To my brain
Entertaining thoughts
That pacify lives pain
This strange day is
Numbed with splendor
A heart pumping out joy
And euphoria that is quite tender
If divine nature doesn't want
Glory to show
Tell me
Why does this extraordinary herb grow
A little now
A little then
Sometimes contradictions are felt
Fate versus freewill
Just what was dealt
Possibly overcome by shuffling the cards
If anything
Spirituality a must
Hierarchy utmost
And with all this I say that I do trust

ELECTRIC JUNGLE

Looking at this world
I see all the abdicated prey
Bewildered survival
There is not much to say
Charcoaled pepper and salt as white as snow
Equates to what appears as grey
Fighting and churning
Just to make ends meet
Mechanical beings portrayed as human
In a barb wired electrical street
Just who is
Which infiltrates itself into who to trust
I am easily being molded
And acknowledging that I could easily bust
Yet this game of life
I refuse to lose
Watch the illicit drunks
Grossly intoxicated with booze
They are ones
That will fall prey to me
I hone in my sights
And a sudden great victory I do see
I greatly enjoy my freedom
With relentless efforts
To always keep
You will do the following
Such as do sheep
No one will obstruct
My path or impede
Sowing survival
Is this all to the necessary seed
Human mice in search
Of invigorating cheese
Licentious land
But there are no pleas
Trying times
There is no escape
Greedy starving vultures
Your soul
They will greedily rape
Existence is more
Than a noun
Verbally and grimly speaking
It is only a frown
Instincts are the drive
Emotions make evidently clear
Steering wheel clenched
Alone I frantically steer
Will I live to see another day
The predators and savage environment make
Me wonder if my spirit would survive bodily death
When will this unwanted question be answered
Watch as I take in my last breath

ESCAPING WITH FORGIVENESS

Limitations nearly overthrown
Armed with needle and thread attempting to flourish
While still having sown
Escaping the escape
A surreal tainted euphoria although
Always will and does end
Streets paved with sanities asphalt
And somewhere all followers drink holy wine
All accreditations of this most unique cult
Although a fork in road with twisted bend
The god's allowing this night to withstand
Pleading for senses real
Accelerating this pace induced upon land
This medication that was prescribed
Maybe your wish to counteract my heartache
Yet interestingly enough I say a planned demise
Or community interests that helped
To act as a reminder for me to revise
Lives scenario and scenery do flash
A menacing scheme
Will I be buried or become spread ash
What am I composed of'
Fortitude construed with winless valor
The ship at dented aluminum sea
Left upon the dock s me being that bendable sailor
Questions do shape
Molding that appears to increasingly modify
Changing my ways
Will fervent fate continue to comply
Disguise as you may
And camouflage the sigh
Evidence of tension
Imprisoning early in life my taunted conscience
Not of any worldly dimension
I attempted to wake this world
Yet was fraudulently labeled as dead
I am glad that you diffused the bomb
That was left ignite and burning inside my head
Juggling carnal vision
Yet contemplating juggling the naked spirit and soul
Do the divisions counting the revisions
And pay cordially at the toll
Negatives can shift to the positive
Desperate and feeling quite lonely
A sanctimonious conflict still allows to give
I admonish through atonement as the only
Utilizing no more with what is defective
Philosophical judging does require
God granting
The face in the mirror you must admire
Conceding with durable elective
Stay focused
At any rate stick to the fight

Consulting with past successes and failures
Understanding God will not forsake whether the matter being wrong or right
I am saying this sternly
As my current condition seems to be very polite

FEAR OR FIDELITY

Wow….All of this feeling equating itself as supposedly something in which to grasp
Immediately and dangerously this blows up in my sentimental face
Immensely and quite overwhelming this is a sea of emotion that I see
And without a boat and 2 paddles
The attracting crashing of the tide within these 4 walls will not leave me be
As I discover myself feeling although not so warm and fuzzy
Is my mind playing tricks- maybe not you could say
Is this an illusion
Obloquy screams back I don't think so
Welcome to what I call the as forefront of mental confusion
A force of the cards so to say unto me
More than an obvious weird obtrusion
For what I am now witnessing is definitely real
A diabolical attack
To me it appears as if a planned chemikill
My was once bedroom has now become a sea
Even if I swim for the shores
Is this refuge in the unsure and the unclear
Who does the stirring
And who manipulates my undeserved fear
I did not plan on this
And my world of 30 minutes ago is what I do miss
I miss it so bad
So bad that I begin to yell and scream
For this is a wide awake pronunciation
A wide awake….. bad d r e a m
I feel as though I am high-staggering and out of sorts
I pray to Christ to understand God and accomplish some relief
In this sea of madness I am drowning without any comforts
Yet never let go of my ordained be
No longer am I stricken
Floating through the waters I am as if diseased cancer
I find the shores as my tears non have run dry
Further not any longer in that escape of catching my breath
I now have oxygen to fill plenty my lungs with its supply
I find dry shore as the whipping waters graze my cause
And if I see tomorrow with its sun and happiness
Embodied I will be and you will witness firsthand the applause
I run through the land \
Tired as time does pass I walk through the woods
I vision and witness a Holy bible
That is opened sanctimoniously to the book of the mankind's beginning being Genesis
Now you and others that were once lost are included is what I read in the text affirmative
And I now gain my wings and fly as I die yet remember that my end was enormous
Wings of gold
Wings of white
Wings construed with black \
Flying off to the heavens in yellow
Heaven now does await
For this end came early
Therefore not too late
Entering now into the promised land
All lives course assimilations seems to be completed
I never fought off the devil in combat with Michael the archangel as interestingly planned

FEELINGS LEFT BEHIND

Allow for me some leeway in this escapade
The party is now completely happily over
Yet now the money hungry tyrants are anxiously looking too get paid
Who is winning this battle though
Or is there a battle any more to hold
My inner voice tames the angels and demons
And is now held abundant in this situation to currently scold
Where is my love now
Just where did she go
Darts in my hand
The dartboard awaits as I begin to throw
No exact strategy
A matter of chance
Hoping for the best
And evaluating the circumstance
My love for my lady is strong
As strong as a wind that could blow over a skyscraper
I write to her frequently and our love is
Shared largely and fairly at a 50/50
Old school logic says this is complete and satisfying
And blunt to say overall pretty nifty
Yet how focused is your mind
Can you remember what you did a year ago?
Are you in a daze?
Too often self indulged
And in a thick corruptible haze?
These tears of the past find me again today
And I am not rehearsing
As such as for a play
This is real
As real as real can get
Place your wages on my honesty
And forthright you would win that bet
Yet was I bestrewed with a curse of immortality
I am beside myself and also my best friend often times
And wondering just what these days is defined as normality
I too have my quirks, psychosis, and neurosis
Yet is this all just o.k. if I maintian these gestures
For more times than not
They are incidental and bring no pleasures
Metaphysical
Disease meets the games of life
Don't leave me behind
I will pave a path to drive on to succeed
Those still interested
Take up and read
I too must have my crops
And dare you to steal my seed
For without my seed harvesting fruit and victory of life
Just what must I do
Coax you to plant my seed, harvest my crop, and toil while I do nothing
For I want to order and cook from my menu
One life is all I have to give

Without my experiences
Only my feelings get left behind
Cold and lonely
Relentless I will eventually fit in the grind

FIGMENTS, FEARS AND FRETS

Schizophrenias ongoing traumatizing tears
Paranoia
Sometimes subsequent with and not relinquishing its impulsive fears
Encroached you find yourself speedily running
Introverted senses collaborate while nervously hiding
Into a world unjust that has treated me misunderstood as perverse
Tremendously steep are its slippery hills as my climb goes sliding
Wake up
If your able
We'll listen to your stories
And provide support as not to fall and keep you stable
Did you think your psychoses was over yet
Hapless truth itself mechanizes with what is totally unfair
Leaving you nearly senseless while abiding to relocate your soul in a fret
If you want to kill me
Do it now is my statement of pleading
But wicked attackers of self and senses be advised
Your own will you are avidly writing and articulately reading
Tried
Tested
And through sanity itself more than true
Suffering yet not quite a noble
Although a mark of this prominence sticks with society as glue
Alter ego
Could this substitute for a series of lethal avenges to destroy
Any ongoing twists of barraging with assaults
Will leave me attacking with valor confidently
As I go forward in the war and later shall gather the total of results
I run to the hall
As I try to permanently escape
My ethereal soul firmly intact
But the clandestine phantom of fears attempt to rape
I am at a point now where I can forgive
As I have done a thousand times over
For he is a brother of forever's infinity
Intimacy finds me in this seven leaf clover
But nothing now I realize is his fault
An intervention with the clergy allowing these gods to listen
I am early so mark me not as default
The great angels of holy absolution to
Cleanse an impure brain, soul, and mind
Occasionally locate those stubborn phantoms
Who never want to let go as they appear always so inclined
Humiliate
Dominate
The light is guided by yesterdays night with the dark
To remind us lively of heavenly sleep
As I was mentioning much earlier
Fears can be gripping and anonymously they do creep
Here is the test
The seed of fertility you'll see does hold this I attest
Upon conception and at that birth
Welcome to somewhere and forever
Agnostic prayer included

We are born, live, die and are buried
I pray that that hope is not refuted
Or disputed
Only commuted
Give me your blood and I'll give you a sometimes uninhabited heart
Because we all know that 1 plus 1 equals 2
Hey bro, who ever said I was that smart

FLYING WITHOUT WINGS

Dull your senses
Relieve your untimely pain
Take salt not by block
Take by grain
Becoming crazy as one of
The frenzied stage
Sufficient love in heart
Forgetting tempering past rage
Reality takes flight
Yet is different than tender dreams
Dirty politics attempting to unveil
Menacing crooked schemes
Do not turn a cheek
Take a stand
Vigilante colleagues
Follow instruction respecting command
Rapidly flying in the air
Strategy applied
Wisdom a cure
Flight safe and responsive
The passengers are sure
Realization now
Ultimately there are no wings
6th sense applied
Religious intervention
And a bellowing monastery sings
Desires captivate
Emotional altitudes help to complex
Deciphering just what is a blessing
And what is a hex
Denominations
Do we take tangled high bid
Or mangy low bid
Or simply take current
Winnings and run
Money and riches
Hide and conceal
Lives chapters- not knowing all
Time does reveal
See the cards dealt
On the bottom of a stacked deck
Near fatal collision
Walk unscathed from the horrific wreck
Be careful in this world
Yet not awkward or timidly shy
Passing the test
All survivors do comply

Fortunes or fallacies of fallen fiction

Destitution
So to say being dirt poor
Obtaining only proverbial knowledge
Prudence although forthright still allows much too explore\
Who cares you say
For this poor and desperate yet quality man
A visionary who only has a few fans or say hosts
Yet within trust is observation faith adhering to a plan
Please courageous soldiers stand firm consequently holding to your posts
What will become
And maybe just who is to say
Silent thoughts pervert and oddly seem to disconnect
Uttering words frequently that appear to always end in nay
Bi-God
Is this world blind to the fact that
Some have been grossly neglected and often cheated
Or is it possible to restore sight in ignorant humanity
Where the once blind, crippled, and diseased have competed
It takes a leader with literate docile compassion
Who keeps his sights set on others not the self
And may even be remarked as a fashion
Is this possibility entrenched within your own pleasure
Because if even just one penny you have freely given
To a desperate soul you may have become that someone's treasure
Ascribe
Do you know what I mean
Not speaking to detriment in obloquy or hocus pocus
Yet to some degree captivation of thought as financial material green
have you ever been so poor
Where you could not afford a thing
No now I am counting my losses
Perpetual harmony falters as I see nothing does bring
I can hear what seems as a birds warbling
And joy reenters my heart simplistic as the crow does sing
A reminder possibly that although by some considered a creep
If I plant my seeds wisely all principles do add up
And I will eventually or instantly make a buck that I can keep
Do not give up my friend
For your days will not end in doom if you keep even minimal belief
Trust your heart
And see to it that victory is absolution of resolution expecting relief
Fortunes or fallacies of fallen fiction
Possibly you do write your own text
Ultimate choice concedes with due respect abstaining from restriction
Care and concern
An effort that I must let you know of
For I believe that you have in accordance completely obeyed
Go ahead now and fly because you are the peaceful dove

GOBLETS OF GOSSIP

He said, she said
I hear the sickening accusation
Innermost turmoil
Contained within this troubled situation
Tongues fork chastising to inflict
Humans resembling snakes
And around my neck constrict
I drink from the gold goblet
The celestial wine of the gods in hand
Contorting my senses
With truth in demand
Inexcusable gossip has
My back to the wall
Innocence I know
Yet refusing to take the fall
Distressing leads me to follow
The steps to forgive
Yet if not followed
May I still gain entrance to eternally live
Quality of mind
Equates to solid mental welfare
Within me are the powers that be
Malice do not dare
Remember this moment
Do not forget this day
Betrayal is an ongoing cheated hand
Elasticity as you know represents flexibility
Because I was rendered without a rubber band
I am alone now
Such as before
Ascending through depths of intuition
And fathoming deep to explore
Stray from gossip
To wash this filth clean
Purity is overcoming my starving soul
Consequently taming my limitless inner voice
Do angels on high look upon
And tabernacle to rejoice
Exempt from crooked fate
Living in the now
Praying it's never too late
War has been waged
Transgressed calculations arrive
Strategies that answer
Mandatory obligation to survive
When push comes to shove
Arms fair and wide open
I'll rise above
Rhetoric dictates the bigger man
Is the one who walks away
And the smaller man unwisely
Engages into the fight
Absolution intervenes with
It's hierarchical sight

My words here indicate
Validity of this circumstance
Vertigo creates thoughts
That both sing and dance
Guidance shines on what is
Heard and what is gainfully seen
This armor is my beacon
Conquering with valor
The enemy apparently does weaken
Immunity sweeps the problem
Underneath that old rug
Injured yet hopeful
Without the need for any drug Yet the need for no drug

HEALING YOUR HURT

What you try to conceal
The hands of time
Carousingly just might reveal
But keep this in mind
Within time most things do heal
This too shall pass
Yet I am saddened at your ordeal
I am not exonerated
Or in jubilation now
Yet I wait at your door
My direction defiantly finds me
In a state of turmoil
Lost within my own soul
Form east to west
And north to south
Pondering with what exactly
Shall flow from my assigning mouth
I see that you are not home
Yet feel your presence
The fog is lifting
And these storm clouds are not as dense
The letter that I leave behind
Confirms my attempt
To have let my love show
My flowers here represent nothing more than sentiment
They shall propagate and grow
Although deprived from sunshine being quite much
And all other essentials promising as food
This a sensation of unique touch
All prominence of fortitude
Nostalgia hits me hard
Maybe being the beginning of
All beginnings
And not the end of all ends
I am with you now as before
And consecration it lends
You can spend time
But cannot buy it back
Life a tug of war
Invaluably you must pick up the slack
Panic drives theses roads
Desperate for a passenger
To frighten and alarm
My thin egg shelled mind
Do not try to break or harm
I will see you soon
In the meantime
Please think of me
Always attempting to free
Your handcuffs loosened
And your freedom is my key
Mentally, spiritually, and bodily
Nothing left to seize
Because purity I really do see in you

Thanks for healing my hurt
And cleansing me with absolution as new
Now you hold the cards as the dealer
And I am sure you know as of what to do
Angels talk to me
They create freedom
How much more do you want to see

HERO OF A FEW

You cry
But visibly with no tears
Civilized protector
In a land that is crude
Save a soul
Rules from heaven above
Disadvantaged aggressor
The focus of love
God's angels now although have
Their ultimate tests
Are they able to forgive inconceivably and rewrite texts
So if followed we are all sanctimoniously blessed
Enemies are much
And pondering with fans just a few
Please erase the slate
For each day now is new
In a domino effect
Watch the days collide
Celestial flying angels
Heaven the final reward
The soldiers do battle
And henceforth die by sword
In hopes the innocent
Shall prosper again
10 commandments
Deliver us from sin
Forever euphoria
Endless smiles
A colossal major attraction
That is traveled everywhere from all miles
The first shall become last
And the last become first
Feeding our hunger
While drinking away the thirst
Never gave up
Says the underdog phrase
Continuing to see the light
Despite the thickened prickly haze
Hero of a few
Maybe your friends are nil
Yet do not let that discomfort you ever
Being the underdog partner-can be an overwhelming thrill
The promised land awaits those very certain ones
Who believed

HIERARCHY OF HEAVENLY HOPE

Is it within me
Or construing divergence possibly within you
Promises nearly broken
And I'm not sure exactly as what to do
Promises hoping to mend
Broken hearts
The candle always nearly diminishes
But with earthly or ethereal vision
Never faltering it always restarts
Trust, love, hopes and dreams
Vanquished nearly
Never trudging useless peace indefinably always reams
Into me
Into you
Love not departing
I am the ratchet and you are the screw
I value a moment as I define sacred as this
And not believe that this love is genuine
Not allowing for thought to become lethargic
Becoming intoxicated within merely a sip of wine
Don't ever dare to neglect
And therefore please do not pervert
Acknowledge past success while turning a cheek
If enemies of thought incessantly remind you of painful past hurt
Hierarchy of heavenly hope
Don't allow others to bring you down
Become a ruler of accredited justice with micrometer to examine descriptive scope
Believe in what you may
Do if you so choose the Lord's will
Efforts at salvaging someone's soul burdening problems
Another effort to understand a not so easily obtained skill
Angels now encompass with divine ways appearing as surreal
Thought and vibrant living synergetic while externalizing emotion
As the pages do turn defining what you now understand does heal
Turning, learning, souring oppression this good heart is churning
The devils in a land harvesting putrid seeds
Not cultivating therefore henceforth not concealing only burning
Prosecute
Refute
Scandals of that nature raping integrity while chasing financial loot
Change your ways
Modify your views
Prospects of what may appear as gainful only seem to lose
Trust for once more than just your own heart
Intentions of this caliber never will fade
Getting to heaven although
I suspect this is not such an easy grade
Love one another indiscriminately
Such as God does love you
Because when walking on glass
You most definitely must have on your foot an impenetrable shoe
Trust within salvation the wish to destroy what is wicked
Because an undying trust within worth of this

Possibly holds while contained a very fortunate ticket
So we'll end this prayer now as long as you now your roll
Inhabitations of character pure with thought resolute equating to what is absolute
Shall rise to glory of expectation with guidance that does extol

HONESTY IS....

Words of spoken tenacity
Are being spoken from a gingerly start
Yet I ask of what do I pertain
So much that I need to get off my heart
Very much I need to explain
Dreams
Am I within the power of persuasion
To show you just what my love does offer
Hypothetically
True emotions perplexing with people of plastic
Analytically
Conclusions drawn that I don't fit in the clique
What will keep me at the norm
My mind is it's own worst enemy
And it seems like brain surgery I should immediately perform
Yet both equate to prove a pondering point
Rapidly losing my faith with supposed Christians
Would God kindly reconcile and anoint
And speak from a heart of virtue
Being shed and kicked down
Show me the light so that I may get thru
Some so greatly granted
Yet some got so cheated
Playing this game without all of the pieces
How so could I have successfully competed
Fate of God at times seems to poison my once sweet
Passion of freewill and chance
Is it still God's angels I follow
I hear the screaming inner voice and take my stance
God can do anything
100 times faster than we can blink our eye
I am listening to find
While we are all in the grind
I must look deep to keep you in mind
I attempt to see the brighter other sides inflection
Open doors
Opportunities coming to you all direction
Not allowing for oppression other's imposed doubt
Feeding the hungry soul at any detection
Look within
For you have so much to offer and give
Life congruent with it's unique experiences
The ultimate answer although is to cordially live
Become familiar with a higher power
Past mistakes hopefully are seen as stepping stones
And henceforth strength meets euphoria which just won't cower
Examine your past
Yet look to the future to see a brighter tomorrow
Stay in touch with emotional amplitude
And gracefully understand this as graceful sorrow
We have been given a unique gift
One that is respondent not with want yet needs
The battle is defined by the relentless yet swift
When the world knocks you down

Get back up and fight twice as hard again
Because even those who were once lost
Find triumphantly ways to earn a win
Lost still within which side although to pick
Is not always so fun
Worries could overwhelm you and as your body stays still
The innocent mind is on the run

HYPNOTIZED

Hypnotize
Strangely enough I now follow my own advice
Hungrily pursuing the pie in the sky
Because even those in last place deserve a slice
How can my plate be although full
When sickeningly enough poverty knows me by first name
Branded
Stranded
Abstaining from adverse worldly influence
Commanded
Whose making my limitations
Demanded
Surreal the light glimmers at tunnels end
Attempting to maintain complete faithfulness
Saddened to see society's aim to apprehend
Secure in your hands this needle and thread
Linking up gross injustices and poignantly mend
Throw back
Surprisingly the guilty are often uncaught fish
While the innocent swim against the tide
Guided and consequently dominated by wish
Just what is your magical charm
Are you bestowed by delusion or fantasy
Expelling what is evil henceforth unable to harm
Bellowing I hear the horns enormous sound
The angels triumphant music significantly does alarm
No sleep inducing pills needed this session
Genuine words indeed represent my despair
Uniquely enough my alter ego rests upon fantasy
And my total package finds my dreams so distant and rare
Theatricals
This art of charades collides with simplistic fun
Chemicals
Unseen by most these substances still catch my eye
Observable twist
Shuffle the deck of cards
A temptation that's tough to resist
No longer an estranged prisoner in mental wards
Bring your own starlight everywhere you go
Although notorious thieves will steal the light
Allowing myself to just not know
Allowing avenging wings to carry me off in flight
Entertain if you may guests within the smallness
Of this little world
And the bigness of our own successes
Adorned as rich or poor
Meekness though does not allow for stresses
Can you not notice though doctor
This is the best way to see inside my head
Visions or merely illusions
This conglomeration of muses definitely does lend
Accepted
The Maker sees that I have instruction
Respected

Informing you of your onward induction
Inflect
The clouds change direction at thought alone
Reject
Subtleness allows the good to speak in soft tone
Open the mind
Close out your misconception
Divine honest articulation
I now see now as a blessed redemption

IMMORTAL YOU

Put your hope in me
A zeal of newfound faith
You will continue to see
You have heard it before
You will hear it again
The life you lead is good
Yet at times is anchored within it's sin
Not good enough for heaven
Yet not bad enough for hell
The prayer that I commune
Without a price I do sell
A foregone conclusion
An ongoing story with much too tell
I demand some justice
And in mutual terms
Delegate order while listening
A method to comfort shattered nerves
Yes a bad hand was dealt
Yet far from begging your sympathy
Vulnerable emotions although are felt
The Almighty Creator allows evil
Yet is not the author of
I view this as exonerating extreme unkindness
And within me this does bother love
We are a kind
That still that does see the light
Maybe a little late
Yet do not allow for unsettling fright
Deprived of thought, word, and action
Not quite sure of how or why
Observable is the twist with reaction
This propaganda is not coincidence
Too many things are evident
Why were we chosen
Obscurity dims yet still prevalent
Pray modern medicine is here for mankind…. and….
Will fix the broken bones
The surgeon sees this as tenable
And with solace she confidently atones
The hurt although is clear
The need for a analgesic
A communion of new souls
Supposedly a infinitely planned clique
I pray this strange world is left eventually
Just to find your going to the next
Meddling with curiosity
We are all - equally sexed
This man prays for a woman
To keep me fulfilled
Keeping you satisfied
I guarantee my efforts to keep you thrilled
Convene in praying
Take this goodness as not being absurd
True I am a lone traveler
Yet enthusiastically still stay close to the herd

INFINITE IS INTELLIGENCE

I try to comprehend
Infinity forever
Heaven or hell
Dwelling places to abode
With infinite stories to tell
Torture and torment
Or loving peace and joy
Dying old man
Or infant with whimsical toy
What is the criteria to enable this employ
Once a human life to this earth is conceived
A soul shall be permanent or say always existent
And this being more than just what is commonly perceived
An infidels ego and also their logic seem to deflate
Birth, live, die, and grave
There is more too expect as I begin too feel irate
I too have spoken to many type agnostic minds
Yet ratio integrity with much more than just hate
Nearly impossible to perceive
A soul that has passed either is descended or ascended
Now there is no charity that allows you to leave
Where do you draw the line
Does a line need to be drawn at all
For the record
Apostle Paul's original name was Saul
Angels, saints, and spirits
These are all inspirations from God
Guarding and protecting
Wings flying
They are able to resurrect
They bring to life
Both miracles and a surplus of love
Holy beings
That fly like a dove
Do not allow for cynicism to drag you
Or push false pretenses into your brain and all about
Even though poor and meek
You my friend have demonstrated colossal clout
Who cares you say
Others say you must
For faith in mankind in itself will fall apart
And from within the structure will rust
Is forever here
Is forever there
Is infinity going to be everywhere
In reverence to clairvoyance
These are my understandings which I needed to share

INFINITY IS WITH US

Within you or others I am not attempting to annoy
Being deemed proper and spiritually respectful to others and self
What is the criteria to enable this employ
Once a human life to this earth is conceived
A soul shall be permanent or say always existent
And this being more than just what is commonly perceived
An infidels ego and also their logic seem to deflate
Birth, live, die, and grave
There is more too expect as I began too feel irate
I too have spoken to many type agnostic minds
Yet ratio integrity with much more than just hate
Nearly impossible to perceive
A soul that has passed either is descended or ascended
Now there is no charity that allows you to leave
Where do you draw the line
Does a line need to be drawn at all
For the record
Apostle Paul's original name was Saul
Angels, saints, and spirits
These are all inspirations from God
Guarding and protecting
Wings flying
They are able to resurrect
They bring to life
Both miracles and a surplus of love
Holy beings
That fly like a dove
Do not allow for cynicism to drag you
Or push false pretenses into your brain and all about
Even though poor and meek
You my friend have demonstrated colossal clout
Who cares you say
Others say you must
For faith in mankind in itself will fall apart
And from within the structure will rust
Is forever here
Is forever there
Is infinity going to be everywhere
In reverence to clairvoyance
These are my understandings which I needed to share

INNER CLOCKS

Inner clocks
Who did the winding
Inner clocks
Interest we are finding
Where does the drive
To succeed really come from
Who is pushing the buttons
And who is pulling the strings
Nobody is calling
Yet the telephone it chaotically still rings
Answering the call is the call of obligation
Despite the sluggishness within
The jungle I see is planet earth
And my survival is a win
Watch the human puppets contort
What is the reason for everything
An expectation of plentiful resort
An intriguing world
Yet littered with broken dreams
Sunlight still shines
And down it beams
The rich got the upper hand
The poor apparently got the hand
With fingers broke
And where there is fire
There is smoke
The inner clocks believably
Guide to exist and procreate
Believe that life begins today
And it'd never too late
Poverty and overwhelming destitution
A kinder road to sympathy and predestination
Maybe the facts equate to evolution
But a conflict in
My mind is revealed
God's healing touch
A wholehearted prayer conveys
To be cured just as much
To give is richer
An artful touch
Paints the picture
Connect the dots
God made your choices
Lives with plots
If you do not believe humans
Have genuine emotions
Than immediately stop feeding and
Watering those wild and exotic green seeds
Planted within those pots
God forbid if it causes any pixilated unforeseen problems
Than just do not include it into an angel's specific garden lots

INTEGRITY

Seems just like another basic day
Variation ensuing and ultimate apex of success looming
Oblivious to this reality it appears as if a fatality
Emotions obscure as to sour just temporarily
Feeling confined yet obviously seeking congeniality
Subtle thought reroutes itself to maddening mania feeling
How to reach for the stars
When inevitably all on top I see is the ceiling
Insufficient financial flow
Broken smile
Am I sane in a world that has went insane within
Or just a reminder of acceptance with often denial
Instantaneous
Success I have learned as others comes with tests
I am my own conscious government and authority
In this selfish land I could make many painstaking arrests
Yet that is not the story
What exactly from this life is it that I desire
And therefore I belong in what category
Trust your gut
Rely on your instinct
For accomplished unity is a blessing
Which the foundation of allegiances are linked
Yet once I have made my mark
Freedom of opportunity still could contain blemish
As I wait patiently to hear just what they embark
Always changing
Never sitting still
Allocating to the win of others as well as self
That is the most harmonious thrill
Retribution
Yet just who is getting paid back for evil deed
Restitution
How can you put a price on all of which that was stole
Smog of the politics equals colossal sometimes as wasted breath
Pollution
How do rate yourself- as decent and quality
The hypocrites only see what is material unfortunately
As they are blinded and obviously choose not to see
You must be resilient
That is the most pervasive thought of dimension
When that statement of simplicity is analyzed
It greatly reduces any yet not all mental tension
Maybe I should not be so tough or hard
When the mind grows faintly alert yet numb
We all want a piece of the pie
And more than just a miniscule crumb
Modify
Change
Only when change need be done
Do not step on souls or bodies to reach the top
Another basic step to free your brain from feeling -it is on the run

Some things are or just merely perceived as prearranged
Yet I am certain
To deliberately fail in this life
Is only yourself that you are hurting

INTRICATE EMOTION
INTRICATE EMOTION

Figment
Solidarity pleads for you to be real
Jubilation partners with kindness
Moving forward through this abstract surreal
A bond with you
Obviously I realize that you sow my path
Promiscuous consecrations from the gods
Never allowing severance and it's untimely wrath
Difficulty is explaining our lives
In a brief synopsis
I will add that my fantasy is your dream
And unconsidered hearts have too much too miss
Games not being played
That could annihilate this bond
Memories of you I hold
And establish roots with idealism fond
What exactly is this emotion
Deepening and conglomerating within the soul
Living only for your love
Watch the scattered dice roll
Hearts that are pure
Comfort renders with time passage to console
Experiencing all facets of love
My steep ticket paid at the toll
You are so sweet
A portrayed spirit with parameters unbound
A once maimed heart now pumps again
A euphonic music billows it's resilient sound
My time spent with you
Does open doors
I welcome opportunity upon the step
Emotionally uplifting
Compilations with an energetic gymnastic pep
I see your world
Yet ask if I am within your galaxy
Where to from here
Another planet I await to accompany and see
An electric blender
Crashes within itself triggering an emotional collage
Crank the speed to high
All I see is fiction and resembles a mirage
A frustrated contentment
Knows me on a first name basis
Painted pictures resemble photographs
Yet are actually distortions of past loves and how passion chases
You help me understand
Together with this emotion we learn to cope
Romance and purity
The tub dances with soap
When the tide does shift
The moon's radiance swiftly crashes the tide
Allowing myself to truly find you

The vast river allows nowhere to hide
Embraced
Held so close
Erased
Pain diminishes
Chased
Cupid's arrow has found me
I will keep praying for your return
That is if you were to grimly ever leave
Without you I am innocently shackled
My intentions bestowed and still I grieve
You are gratifying light
You are my illustrious intention
You are my right
<u>Is truth revealed</u>

It all comes out in the wash
Subtleness of time passing pervades altruistically
Secrets to be revealed
The crowd of chosen followers runs blind temporarily
But with this truth obtainable their fate is sealed
Deceptions
Receptions
What lies beneath
So compelling it steals your thought
As an angry voice mutters behind the teeth
Suspicion lies at the doorsteps unknowingly while
Grim hope shows your utter resignation
Partnerships that prove far from loyal
Wondering who is who
And caught seemingly endless within the vast turmoil
Armed with compass and map yet strangely without direction
Now thereafter just what to do
I smell a rat surfacing the odor not the only detection
Within what secrets does honesty contain
Living this life of dirty laundry exposed
Yet some say still say my belief is all in vain
Dejection
Correction
May you hear and speak only truth of me
This aversion allows only for bad memories to remain intact
Yet divine nature return with soundness the ability to flea
You reneged on your offer to keep this unsaid
I shall retract back to my world with feelings not yet settled
I attempt to put aside shame as I walk amongst the dread
No vengeance within me no not as of yet
Yet I revamp upon all of this guess work
And I am not sure with it just when I will get
A second chance
When my first chance should have not been dismissed
.The game of mental calculations with strategy utmost
I see certain qualities omitted from this moderate list
When a deception is thrown
Darkness of lies tarnishes
Allowing that vindicator to cast from his corrupt throne
Just what is left to do
What is the retaliation

Sneaking in seeds of salvation
Upon the cultivated plantation
Because I also have deceived and lied and such
A 50-50 dinner treat if you will
Pleasing to see the return of the favor same as the dutch
My past doggedness carouses the opportunity to forgive
Foundations of what I call true values
So that we all may coexist and onwardly live
Business can be bloody in the figurative
Yet still unique and illustrious form
Stay away from what is hidden vile and corrupt
Although you see this as a mainstream norm
Create your own rules broken one so you do not forcibly erupt

JUGGLING EMOTIONS

Intentions
Inventions
Theses being creations of thoughtful mind
Yet allowing for recovery of procedure of event
So much time spent
Yet nothing but this valuable gift was lent
Open the box
To live in the present
Difficult and perplexing to fathom
For the change of day to modern day peasant
Love
The newborn definitely does adhere
Relinquishment of pure and absolute body
Pieces of the soul unite which is impervious to fear
Welcome to this overlooked commodity
Changing of the seasons
Coexists symbolically with the changing of time
Maybe referring back to yesteryear
The chimney smokes as neighborhood church bells chime
It is nice to feel complete and unimpaired
Despite days of darkness
When daunting voices internally screamed that nobody cares
Ritual
Habitual
Not missing the mark by much
Staying much beyond active in this goal
Yet reflecting at days gone past
Many times I never understood my role
Mixed sorrow
Obviously it stands it's chance for rebirth
Consequently the goal is to create contentment
Yet understand emotions and their euphoric worth
Isolation
Procreation
Intricacy of vast mind with choice
If the proper steps are taken
The Saint's guiding hands allows me to rejoice
So take these small steps
Take them upon your enlightening escapade
Hopefully your colors are full and vibrant
And consist that possibly of jade
Juggling the past with the present
Also the today which is greeting the unknown
My eyes encompass the range of feelings
And somehow these blossoming seeds planted have grown
Pristine to say the least is wonderful at margin reward
This war has been ceased
Undying relentless effort allows me to drop my sword
Life
Sometimes too much too hold
Actions
Always enough too mold
Victory\
Your victory is sweet to the taste

Yet engagement of war usually
Equals only as complete and utter waste
Be strong as an ox and attempt to not confuse
Because people will try to throw you off course
Yet fortitude is nearly a requirement to not ever lose
I miss
You miss
Please understand
Life although unpredictable
Still intervenes with the soul as being in command

LEAVES DO TURN OVER

Pleasure and pain
Pain and pleasure
Withstand or collapse
Just what signifies a quality building of architecture
Obviously I despise my wasted years
Yet now in humor laugh at the agonizing stress
Not holding back with inane yet completed expression
Inspiring words to boldly confess
Running out of people to blame
Misfortunes too I once did hold
Trying and apologetic stories from the old
Push to the top
Never give in
Break free from bondage
And just do not compromise with sin
Please do not cry for me
Yet appreciate my worth
For I to have hungered on
This plentifully harvested earth
I try not to look back
And march forward being the
Second hand on the clock
Years do compile frantically
The noise beckons….tick tock tick tock
My mind is growing stronger
As my body is growing tired
Impossible to get fired or quit
If the maker is he who has hired
I believe in a hierarchy if you will
A subtle twist
To govern my life with extreme light
The candle remains lit
Even in the dead of night
My cries can not be heard
But observable are my tears
A puddle of emotion
That is transgressed with emotion and ultimately fears
Do not neglect others
Conceit sees the self as number one
The hateful shoots bullets
Yet watch the peaceful steal the gun
The best prayer is the one that
Did go without an answer
Or may I say that of a cure
Succulent food accompanies the feast
And within my mind methods do stir

LESSER GOD

One third of the once holy ordained
Now meeting it's monopolistic jealous rulers own
As for nature and mankind yet just what to do
Unforgiving God -and to his ultimate tester to reverse his throne
God crashes with no compromise or treaty of peace allowed
A true unique open minded straight to the point inking
And convinced new followers take up systemizing while vowed
The stars of the galaxies not left out are winking
God green
Of peace
Of money to necessitate a giving truth
For all know these plans have been transcribed before the womb
Yet far from being a super sleuth
Yet a life so bizarre they already created my tomb
God green
Green is our color
A tint of black, white, red, and blue I suppose
Sometimes agonizing mind games of what we dislike
Puts you in the situation of ....you knows
What color attacks-what is supposed to be the holy ones
They turn their Ouija boards instead to the skies
And its ultimatum is owned by nuns
Job and Jesus
Follow these words
Do exactly and only as the Almighty does wish
Or either with torture, death, or disease
Shall you going with punishment or I could abolish
What has been unfairly targeted as bad
Has indeed true meaning of good
What about the trials and tribulations of God himself
The ultimate game player-how can never lose
Our colors now become black and blue?
Yes, because if you get in God's way-he shall eternally bruise
Lucipher
Leader of the angels fall
Actually is in attempt to put in the 4th season
And that 4th season was titled fall
Not better than God- though Lucipher did plead
Just forgiveness for Adam and that
Tempting apple that some called our virtue of sin
This story not being pretty
As I carry myself stern and chagrin
God demanded
God disbanded
And yes he is a jealous God
Therefore a sinning God himself you should say
As you know-God despises jealousy
It's internal manifestation- being both sick and very prevalent
Similar to that of the disease Leprosy
Give accreditations to these words
For they are true I must say
I also pray to God such as the wailing Lucipher, Jesus, and Job did
Yet as for my gainful existence
I have become as a termite that you just can't rid

The holy bible yes is a coded book
But a coded book is rules to a game
That to an extent keep on changing
Deranging
Supposedly new thought exchanging
When does the world end
When does the better world begin
Come on do the math
Fate , freewill, circumstance or sin
What did the prehistoric dinosaurs from the past's in

LESSONS IN LOVE

I suppose I could study these here books
My whole life and not understand what love is
Have you noticed the academic scholars in school
Usually fail in love and prosper in other academics as a wiz
Please forgive me
If my views seem nearsighted
Never do I want to arrange a situation
Where you feel as if you are plighted
We all deserve what I say is necessary love
And therefore love deserves us all
A situation annealed with pain
As an adversary yet we here your dialing call
Don't neglect
Please appreciate the meaning of respect
See the metal leaves fall
From the tree garbed in silver and gold
Is this maybe another anonymous fable
That is weathered and really quite old
Lessons in love for both
Nature and mankind to believe
View the crystal ball
Is this fact or illusion or just what I oddly enough perceive
Innocence finds the toddler
And mysterious is everything
Within it's grasp
The sandpaper firms to wood
With an abrasive rasp
Yet it does not cut or
Promote into decay
An exuberating feeling the perplexed
Experience when utterly dismayed
A day without love
Compares to a bird that just cannot fly
Your distant cries
I could never erase or nullify
Quieted contentment carries itself meagerly
Often as only a societal sigh
A nameless feeling exalts the
Simplicity of a human touch
Despite the wreckage of the accident
The bones heal without any crutch

LIFE'S COURSE

If you had just one wish
What would it be
Are you in chains
Or would you say you are free
Do you ever find
Yourself falling in love
Or downtrodden climb in hate
I don't believe either in destiny
Yet translated possibly through fate
Theism not divine revelation
Possibly narrates your book
Venturing amongst the trails
While being vested in the nook
Evil is what should be thrown away
Roaming in this spirited land
I welcome each new day
No time for tears
No time for remorse
All delusion factors that set in
And currently throw me off course
Everybody strange to say
Must stands this worlds test of time
Did you for forget the compulsion
The opposite reacting antecedent that spells climb
I know
I know
Do not become besieged without
The power of self focused and ever necessary love
Life itself is cards you did mention
Without all of the fifty two though
Does it bring the game to a new dimension
Play wisely with what you were dealt
Although too I am vulnerable
As intimate emotions true emotions are felt
What is it exactly that you want to achieve
Look deep within too find the answer within
The pits utmost corners of loves valleys
I would place all bets your life would not reflect
The drunken vagrants down on the streets ally's
Sometimes fame and fortune
Are a sure bet to succeed and strive
Maybe a wish to be left alone and have nothing
Just in itself happy to be alive
Rules my friend for all of all
Have been broke
Such as the new world bible leaders
They are adorned in their subtle cloak

LIFETIME GUARANTEE

Be yourself
Become numb to the games
The delivered become free
Excerptions of biblical claims
But please remember this
Secret phrase
Never let down your guard
Or you could regret
All of your coming days
Grit your teeth
When people toy with you
And your heart begins
To radically bleed
Turn and plant
The immortal infinite seed
I have been left behind as others
Daily bread although has been consumed by greed
Looking onward
My intuition steadfastly continues to grow
No egos are broken or shattered
So on goes the show
Focus and keep sight
An honest virtue should not be misguided
For if legitimate and forthright it is not a plight
Please keep your soul, body, and spirits
And brain intact
The quarterback is scrambling
And although efforts true may be sacked
Romantic dreams
Sell at a dozen for a dime
The wind is howling and restless
Yet outside the angelic church bells chime
Just what human eye can judge
What the interested eyes do see
Interest soars
The final verdict
Never to be revealed inside those locked secure doors
Mystery is the books
Honesty is stolen
Theft occurs from both imposters and crooks
Remember happiness involves
The undying pursuit of freedom
And bondage
To any, way , of anyway
Should not be attached
Yet from all the battling and fussing
My skin isn't wretched or permanently scratched

LIVES COURSE

If you had just one wish
What would it be
Are you in chains
Or would you say you are free
Do you ever find
Yourself falling in love
Or downtrodden climb in hate
I don't believe either in destiny
Yet translated possibly through fate
Theism not divine revelation
Possibly narrates your book
Venturing amongst the trails
While being vested in the nook
Evil is what should be thrown away
Roaming in this spirited land
I welcome each new day
No time for tears
No time for remorse
All delusion factors that set in
And currently throw me off course
Everybody strange to say
Must stands this worlds test of time
Did you for forget the compulsion
The opposite reacting antecedent that spells climb
I know
I know
Do not become besieged without
The power of self focused and ever necessary love
Life itself is cards you did mention
Without all of the fifty two though
Does it bring the game to a new dimension
Play wisely with what you were dealt
Although too I am vulnerable
As intimate emotions true emotions are felt
What is it exactly that you want to achieve
Look deep within too find the answer within
The pits utmost corners of loves valleys
I would place all bets your life would not reflect
The drunken vagrants down on the streets ally's
Sometimes fame and fortune
Are a sure bet to succeed and strive
Maybe a wish to be left alone and have nothing
Just in itself happy to be alive
Rules my friend for all of all
Have been broke
Such as the new world bible leaders
They are adorned in their subtle cloak

LOVES CAPTURE HAS SECRET DIGITS

Quite overwhelming to say the minimum of word
Will I find a soul mate to help unlock my heart which contains multitudes of love
Or is what I profess or perceive more than just completely absurd
I renew myself and stay mindful to games and sinister tricks of this land
Sometimes it appears as if the only connection I can make is time through an hourglass
It is difficult to camouflage heartache of yesteryear with only just sand
Although I search
And I definitely do seek
This red wine in hand seems to comfort me as a remedy
Yet strangely out of my brain the possible solution anchoring incredibly does leak
Always within me instilling this lecture anchoring with intelligence I do confidently see
Freewill entertains my mind to desperately speak
When will I nestle and caress within romance and love
Or will I go unintentionally without
Will my track record hold its own weight
And will I or will I not understand what love is all about
Despite my living contradiction I still do not accept past failure
Because my thick headed mind is made up
Rest assured I hope to follow up with God's infinite tour
I there a lady to unlock my heart of love
Even though I may appear sometime as boldly strong
Needful as I am I may require that bothersome shove
So I do not go abruptly wrong
I will not allow myself to settle any longer for hand me downs
Or what others call a lucky distant second place
Because I did not enter this world to purposely ever fail
Doing so creates a sick and menacing mind prison
And others I suppose would call this residing in jail
So come on
Find me now lover
For I am genuine, real, and a definite to the credit word sincere
I abolish all components of danger, sickened emotion and terror
Or what the majority call as fear
I need love
I desire love
I run after love
Because I suspect
That love often times does run after me
We shall both win the race
A tie being impossible because a split second difference does see
I stand for doing good deeds
And ultimately hope to find a love that is genuinely true
If I am not able to achieve this
I will go back to the start and shall continue on doing what I do
If your love ever does die or blatantly becomes dormant
Realize it is only a temporary setback
Because although love is opposite of hate henceforth use hate to motivate
And not to deteriorate then I believe you just won't lack
Love is real
And it feels so pleasantly good
If in your life you do not feel it
Then definitely right now you should

LOVE QUEST

Embraced
You hold me so close
And bodily very near
Emotional and physical love
Evident and absolutely clear
Moments that are cherished
Reflect memories that always remain
Because consequently this is euphoria
And temporarily remedies lives pain
Such as before
I see you as a divine source
A collaboration of essentials
A unique and benevolent force
This love will never end
I suppose that you just might agree
Ingredients that fit
Harmony comprises this recipe
True love
Does wait on others
An enchanting feel
Freely given to sisters and brothers
Foundations of romance
Seeds that solidify their root
Being void of contamination
And other qualities that definitely do pollute
What is the meaning of love
Look deep within for the inner voice
That whispers an obscure answer
Walking barefoot on flames of fire
Abolishment of fear guides the dancer
Yet love should not baffle
Or choose the upper hand
Tell tale propaganda
Pixies do dwell in this mysterious land
Guidance adhering to love
In actuality serves as a beacon of hope
Wondering makes clear
The proper time to elope
Yet a question does float within
My head with which I do ponder
If you were to leave
Would I be left to continually wander
Will you be there
Forever on my side
I will return all favors
With zero secrets to hide
Can't you see
A fool does not open
Opportunities knocking door
Fabrication of doubt
Leaves nothing remaining to explore

LUDICROUS LIES

It all comes out in the wash
Subtleness of time passing pervades altruistically
Secrets to be revealed
The crowd of chosen followers runs blind temporarily
But with this truth obtainable their fate is sealed
Deceptions
Receptions
What lies beneath
So compelling it steals your thought
As an angry voice mutters behind the teeth
Suspicion lies at the doorsteps unknowingly while
Grim hope shows your utter resignation
Partnerships that prove far from loyal
Wondering who is who
And caught seemingly endless within the vast turmoil
Armed with compass and map yet strangely without direction
Now thereafter just what to do
I smell a rat surfacing the odor not the only detection
Within what secrets does honesty contain
Living this life of dirty laundry exposed
Yet some say still say my belief is all in vain
Dejection
Correction
May you hear and speak only truth of me
This aversion allows only for bad memories to remain intact
Yet divine nature return with soundness the ability to flea
You reneged on your offer to keep this unsaid
I shall retract back to my world with feelings not yet settled
I attempt to put aside shame as I walk amongst the dread
No vengeance within me no not as of yet
Yet I revamp upon all of this guess work
And I am not sure with it just what I will get
A second chance
When my first chance should have not been dismissed
.The game of mental calculations with strategy utmost
I see certain qualities omitted from this moderate list
When a deception is thrown
Darkness of lies tarnishes
Allowing that vindicator to cast from his corrupt throne
Just what is left to do
What is the retaliation
Sneaking in seeds of salvation
Upon the cultivated plantation
Because I also have deceived and lied and such
A 50-50 dinner treat if you will
Pleasing to see the return of the favor same as the dutch
My past doggedness carouses the opportunity to forgive
Foundations of what I call true values
So that we all may coexist and onwardly live
Business can be bloody in the figurative
Yet still unique and illustrious form
Stay away from what is hidden vile and corrupt
Although you see this as a mainstream norm
Create your own rules broken one so you do not forcibly erupt

MAD DOG CREATION

Beware the bites worse
Than then the ravenous bark
Hocus Pocus say the analysts
Yet just what is your remark
The drunken kids engage in childlike antics
And are scandalous at the park
Mad dog creation
What does expound or expand
To the next generation
Hum drum stuff in the papers
Violence on the televisions
Politics and games of divisions
Air time delays and time voids
And only always meet their suspicions
Getting confused
Foaming at the lips
A world without sacrifice is only anarchy
And is coming fast such as the looming Apocalypse
Reveled in overcoming
The skeptics do enquire
Revered by some even as a god
Goal being to get to a status role higher
Is he an icon
Observations of a idol
Make our problems seem so small
And overall abundance of health so vital
Applied science
Seems an alliance
Of beating the odds
Such as defiance
Whose to say
What is intended aggravation
Malicious souls
Find pleasure sickly in other's pain
Applied detergents to cleanse
But it still leaves it's stain
The hungry wolf
Also must survive
The sheep so scatter in attempt
To run their lives course
Zodiak being astrology significant and complacent
And believably is protected by the Taurus
Are you one to demand
Philosophy applied to selections
What is in your hand
Or do peering eyes have infallible predilections
Heaven is tabulated and it's actions
And beliefs are what conduce the list
Yet others in contention say it's just a mad dog creation
That in itself is just too much too resist

MAGIC AND THIS HERE MIRACLE

Fragile frustrations force fascinations of faith
Yet without mechanisms such as these
Just on what basis would miracles have chance to stand
Or beyond understanding if miracles were merely sold
Who be the bearer of this significant brand
And within this would it have books of religion to readily unfold
Divine intervention into both nature and human affairs
The Lord's miracles are untimely and go often irretrievably
But encouragement of the blessed salutations prove the Maker cares
Kindness in excess yet shall I say I say never in profusion
Don't worry your eyes are not playing tricks on you
For sanity's sake alone miracles are not falsified illusions
Pious
Please don't be bias
Try us
Workings of God's kingdom infinitely gleans it's hope
So therefore don't deny and put up a fuss
It may not falter although is in faltering human hands
I hear my calling
Therefore will follow the fundamental commands
To cure
To abstain what does obscure
For we can't therefore we must endure
Is this a right, a promise or neither
I am now in steadfast prayer for I am not quite sure
Is this the supernatural
And completely beyond human understanding
An environment far from being pure
Violence, sex and drugs
It is difficult for me to stay faithfully animate
Yet hopes of a blessed miracle
I am in prayer tonight to get
I now know prayer does not discriminate
For I have been hanging in there
And will bring in the reward as of the painstaking wait
Rich or poor
Young or old
Either somber or filled with luminous light
Miracles are small tokens from heaven
For they always pack a strong punch in the fight
Have you ever had a miracle in your life
One that you could touch, taste, feel and was within sight
Wings on the angels shoulders get snug
And you could imagine that they become immense and tight
Pray for all creation
Both for saints and sinners
Carried on with a confident meekness
The true substance of Christian winners
I pray that you receive your miracle soon
I don't especially want to see those tears
Yet contentment still does understand this sorrow
I think I have received a fair share of fortunate miracles
And what is left over I plead for you to readily barrow

MISUNDERSTOOD

Apparently I am trapped in this abyss call it my own personal hell
Undeservingly-although you have got me all wrong
This is why animosity itself has vacancy and room to rebel
Nobody seems to care about a brother like me
Tarnished and rusted steel
Preponderance of thought induced action
Uniqueness of love renders way to absolution an enchanting feel
Obviously I must stay strong and believe in theism or whatever
Because having a joker up the sleeve may seem interesting
But for targeting a win is always deemed as something very clever
Even though I am not defiled
The blood in my pumping heart appears to be blemished and not quite pure
My faltering hidden heart unnoticed and unseen by medical surgeons
As another day passes and my mind is oblivious and readily obscures
You ask yourself
What is my point
What is my goal
To be given a chance to say the least
And to be driven with Almighty God given soul
What is the course of actions to secure my dreams
If we are adversely afflicted indifferently
Fingers point that we are not on the same teams
All alone and by myself or so the expression goes
Contemplates that border with intrinsic frustration
Playing my cards therefore likewise the dartboard awaits
I am a trooper rock hard to the core courage so I will complete my lives duration
Divine intervention
Will God's holy angels open the eyes to those blind cheating fools
Speak to others directly
So indirectly their laud will speak to me indirectly
Consequently enough my friend
I will get to the point and let you know that I play correctly
So please do not misconceive
Life, liberty and pursuit of happiness
I will mix-up the cards and reshuffle if denied- yet I will achieve
Stretch the truth to a minimum miniscule amount that is what I did
But I have learned if you pass wrongful judgment upon me
Cliché oxy-moron credentials will be attributed
As you are in that jail and I the warden hold the skeleton key
Fizzle
Drizzle
Do not sight of ambition or better yet your dream
Make most of your day and rise in the morning to that whistle
I am glad that you were able to mollify
That much I am just not able to deny
A tear drop falls yet I see it as a solitary cry
So stock up on sufficient quantity and meet your supply
Even if it is only just salvation of your soul do not allow it to be construed
Because yes I enjoyed cathartic times of seemingly endless joy
Yet more days without
Which equals synopsis of immortalizing heartache which I do employ
Understand me
Do not command me
Occasionally such as you also do fail
So kindly please reprimand

My hidden buried heart

Speculation in this notorious hidden town
Has me no longer playing classic case buffoon
True although maybe I was just like you
Not quite right but you still called me crazy as a loon
Infatuation a once was love for life became dormant and swept away
My passion although for life did end and off now to heavens vastness
A catastrophic end even though I love you is what I wish to say
Better off animatedly falling behind
Compared to catering to a jealous preprogrammed world
And disintegrating mentally as a slave to the grind
You people took destiny out of these hands
Even I was believably spiritual
Gave me all your fundamental precedents with commands
Now your E.M.S team has unearthed me maybe to find without heart or soul
Ubiquitously mission impossible even with the women has followed demands
Do you remember me
Listen to the stereo and in reflection or whatever else
At least please remember , and love me, just love me
For I loved and have loved
Yet throwing the dice always incessantly threw snake eyes
Hell here
Hell there
Do the mathematics and you'll find the key won't fit
Hopes of heavens angels to find my once my fraying heart
To find a believer such as me just to get thru
Marionettes, puppets, toys we maybe are of Christ
If my mind appears blasphemous forgive if it begins to strew
Scattered
Tattered
Ripped in two
Shattered
Nothing left to do
Infestation
The only force I use in large numbers were the short
Numbers of my tarnished days instead
By candle hoping to sew my life together in correction
And connectedness yet never having ample thread
In the shadows yet the light caught me separating
Yet I cannot deny the existence of
Not negating
Realize that life is valuable for all
Exacerbating
All colors as if in a prism
Schism
A division within a religious denomination
Or just beg my past life for more
Mutually antagonistic factions or just conglomerations
A situation of ambivalence is in store
Welcome to the spirits and God's world
Which has it's overactive prevalence
I could see my life of happiness was too short
That even though wanting to
Things just would not change
Only derange

A new effort to the explanation of strange
Now I take being quiescent to the next degree
Will the heavens hopefully await
I venture to say yes and soon shall see

My path

Meticulous
Ridiculous
I am desperately hoping theurgy will still apply to my life
Some of which is arbitrated within my own minified mind
This being the final equation of strife
What to accept
And yet just what to decline
Red flags appear suddenly yet in pacified form
Issues of the human mind are noticeably
Elevated when choosing of my bellowing voice
So to say quieted redemption of processional logic
I now see the power of this bold choice
Onward with existence this tight rope just walking won't end
Tribulations along with the trials
Time on your side watch processes begin to mend
On the fence currying favor with the winds
May you fall on the side of security and good
Understanding I have been tried and tested
Strong virtue presents fortitude and is not misunderstood
In clever ways using deception the enemy shall attack
Strategies being education with propriety and they do unite
And momentarily the battle avenges back
I am obviously devising ways to win
May the light see you through
Doors on your path may get shut
Intuition allows a path exacting what to do
Take a look around
So many are caught within themselves only
Working completely for self gain without faith
Yet consequently though sinking and lonely
What drives a strong will to accomplish and succeed
The drive is always changing from person to person
Articulate these words understanding intricacy to proceed
Integrity values very high and the focus of an internal read
Who to follow
Who to trust
What steps to take
The premium makings equal man created from dust
If you so choose
Religion and higher powers keep foundation and their roots
Yet keep this in mind
Even the blessed taste the sweet along with sour
Immaculate minds
Sometimes lead to faltering and idle hands
The effort possibly is to synchronize the two as one
And see just what it commands
Keys that unlock the senses alike
A toddlers first steps or a child on bike
My path is I hope a win
You must be free
And you will

MY PERSONAL GARDEN OF FORGIVENESS

Too long now I have attempted to be free
You have me in your sights and it is extremely difficult with this major distraction
To quite honestly ever to possibly let freedom see
Yet thank our God Almighty for the word and meaning of contradiction
Because without this understanding I just might be ….well….
Nothing more than a living restriction
I will fight to be free and be provocative to the statement of this….
A seed in the garden of freedom has been planted
My mixture of elements has been poured and been visibly decanted
Now for the rest of the gardens delight
Hoeing, raking, and other procedures timed so to say
Not perfect, but what I would call right
The seeds were laid first, now I am at the last step of the gardens serenade
If any green weed somehow does sprout
It was forthright by accident and not my intention of getting harvests paid
Now I realize that the fight of a life
Is in actuality the life of a fight
Without some kind of conflict or problem proliferating
Would or would it not be possible for me to get it right
Take a hit
Blow out the smoke
Rhetoric finds me and you the same
And that in certain ways we are able to joke
Do you need to feel love or the detonation of hate
Come on now
Time is precious so do not wait
It is all good to make a righteous claim
If you want to silence the beckoning beast
Then likewise you have to also learn how to tame
Not for the condition of anything more
Than earning ultimate humility as your fame
You do not always need to lash back to win a war
Harboring on the shadows is peace somewhere
And you have to see more for what is in store
Religion is good
God is great
Enter into absolution
Then you will never be late
For yes there is time for everything and everyone
Let it be free
And let it be not calloused yet let there be fun

My World Is You

Without you
My world is incomplete
Crowded world
But you saved me a seat
To be near you
I would walk from both
Ends of the earth
Keen and avid
How to await our child's birth
When I am with you
Love is so much
Infinite dreaming
You have got the touch
You take away the pain
That this land does bring
Cupid's arrows been launched
But I feel no sting
Heavens guarantees
Make forever appear bliss
Always close; near you
There is nothing to miss
As the years fly by
Your beauty continues to grow
Life is a movie
And I am enjoying the show
Euphoria times infinity
Almost impossible to comprehend
To my loved ones
Prosperity is the
Letter that I send
Forgive mankind's mistakes
And sometimes cruel heart
Complicated dreams
With no end
Yet no start
For you I give
My everything
And utmost beautiful desire
Sunshine with rain
Shall put out the blazing fire

NIGHTMARE BECOMES TOLERABLE

A gingerly yet cautious walk
This tragic nightmare not yet wakened
So abidingly it still does stalk
Into my life now and what was
Reserved time supposed to be supposedly of dreams
A misunderstood soul gets ravished always
And on the inside even salvation lonely itself screams
It's not that I don't accept God
It has just went apparently that God doesn't accept me
A foundation of destitutions nothingness represents my empire
As I always strived for more for me to see
You shall see me again when gone in flesh and blood
My soul and spirit and possibly ubiquitously watching you
Seven leaf clover exhibits total infinity specialized with bud
What is this
Visualizing this as being both a blessing and a curse
This world runs sometimes only by lies
And I receive my stress relieving agents via the nurse
Sympathy and respect I request for me and yourself
Freewill teachers of this land stole destiny books out
Of My marbled black and white shelf
Now in either fantasy, delusion or figment
My only ongoing visits are from Santa's elf's
It's not that thru attraction I could not see
So many woman played me as their personal fool
But overall you attraction just wouldn't see me
Misunderstood
Yet maybe I should abstain and not sell out
Brothers understanding infinity dwell in the hood
Such as paranoia
Love often me
And ever so often so quickly leaves
When does this nightmare given to me evened
And for the pages of life's book become weathered
Are they so badly damaged that won't even bend
Am I speaking in tongues
For believers oriented according to all ethnic\groups to comprehend
Necessity of euphoric dreams in and or out of my life
Is this what I hope someone, some entity or higher power to send
I have prayed
And yes I have hoped
I have self scrutinized
And also have doped
Dreams of heaven undoubtedly solace and comfort
Line your army and I have endured just as much pain and hurt
And for whatever reason I am not exactly sure
Watch the days compile like falling dominoes and watch
As quickly they become lost within the parody and fall into a blur

Of hype and hope

Politics
Innuendos, trickery, and deceit
Blatant and often times fraudulently corrupt
Be sure to save your receipt
Marketing and selling
Equal the bid to make a trade
Emotions allow attached values
Possibly allowing the price to be paid
Despite this absurdness my inner self does entertain
An impoverished candlelit fantasy
Finding itself bordering between joy and pain
I too have repeated the same mistakes expecting
New results yet claiming I am sane
Find not reluctantly this to be a story of love
Not coming up short and exemption of fault
Examine all what is around
To see angels hovering being splendid result
A contented sigh of relief
Contrived and revised
Yet unexpectedly befuddled within
Breaking yet never abolishing
The inner walls of selfish sin
Human nature though devises plans
For this difficult task to not yet plummet
Greed attacks our ambushed personal characters
Yet fervent in climbing up the frosty summit
You can run from problems
Problems that viable sin does bring
A warbling night owl sings as she
Allows a new day dawning to cling
Living in the today
Is not always easy to do
The foot being calloused and small
And colossal is the shoe
Empathy
Walk in these shoes to see what is tough
Sympathy
This worn shoe concludes tattered the path was rough
Sworn to religion and it's view at birth
Encompassing this soul as the ultimate test
Although If not written in what am I
I cry and the tears have confessed
Fools run abruptly to be cleverly deceiving
Such claims as concrete balloons flying
Hocus-pocus convincing as people are believing
Ghosts
Did you hear and see what you you thought
Poltergeist intervention
Observation the expendable method to be taught
Connect the dots
My life is similar to yours
Vacancy of hearts with obtained oceans and seas
Yet clinging to life and swimming for shores

OUTSIDE LOOKING IN QUITE DEEP

City streets littered
With living human debri
The Almighty is looking upon us
But just what does he see
Desolate souls
They strive just to
See another sunrise
Poverty; destitution
Begging for answering
Do you know their resolution
Outside looking in
With wants that are
Merely others needs
A societal cut
And deep is its does bleed
Troubled youth
Seeking answers
Yet not finding the truth
A hooligan for the today
Yet what will it bring
Of the tomorrow
Unpredictable future
Beit although joy or sorrow
Afraid to shed a tear
Lacking remorse
I have become lost and confused
With my lives course
No life is short
That things can't turn around
Limited understandings accompany mental disease
The occasion arrives
And the believers are praying on bended knees
Lack of desire
Periods of hell on earth
Although without burning fire
Be brave and lend a hand
Time fills the hourglass
Yet I see I'm plagued with too much sand
The moment is now
The time has arrived
The world is deviating
The pot has been stirred lets see who has survived
Precious human lives are at stake
Do not turn your back
And malice with forsake
Educate the wounded body
And fill with embodied soul
If not
Pestilence becomes untimely epidemic and takes its toll

OUTSIDE LOOKING IN

City streets littered
With living human debris
The Almighty looking upon us
But just what does he see
Desolate souls
They strive just to
See another sunrise
Poverty; destitution
Begging for answering
Do you know their resolution
Outside looking in
With wants that are
Merely others needs
A societal cut
And deep it does bleed
Troubled youth
Seeking answers
Yet not finding the truth
A hooligan for the today
Yet what will it bring
Of the tomorrow
Unpredictable future
Beit although joy or sorrow
Afraid to shed a tear
Lacking remorse
I have become lost and confused
With my lives course
No life is short
That things can't turn around
Limited understandings accompany mental disease
The occasion arrives
And the believers are praying on bended knees
Lack of desire
Periods of hell on earth
Although without fire
Be brave and lend a hand
Time fills the hourglass
Yet I see I'm plagued with too much sand
The moment is now
The time has arrived
The world is deviating
The pot stirred let's see who has survived
Precious human lives at stake
Do not turn your back
And malice with forsake
Educate the wounded body
And fill with embodied soul
If not
Pestilence epidemic could take it toll

PAINTED PICTURE OF POISE

You are a canvass painted with energetic beauty complete
Always rendering judgment that is fair and kind
Key essentials of those logically discreet
Influence
Just enough tint proves that your colors are vibrant and true
Which allows loyalty and a symbol of what to do
Carrying yourself with qualities that truly do uprightly appeal
Yet where do you favour and favor your credentials
Are you a fortress or fortitude of the meaning zeal
So what is your recipe that is so precise
Ingredients containing sunshine and warmth
A cotton candy pleasure indulgingly nice
The groceries contain love and are
Within your loaded grocery cart
Strangely new friendships to myself
Sadly enough often early depart
A candy that is difficult to savor
It likens to sugar yet spoils as tart
When burdened with decisions
See them as forming the ultimate choice
Remember often times the pilot
Is the provocative inner voice
Mending any mistakes I request for fabric and needle
Although rusted and flimsy
Somehow this needle isn't supple to bend
Some see life as a continual tight rope walking act
Unfortunately the unstable fall
Not always being exact that is actual fact
My needlework shapes that of ink
An ocean of a hundred ship
But tragically some inevitably will sink
Speaking figuratively
Lives pages never do end
A chapter that does descend
Allows only for much more to lend
Sanity
Profanity
Cursing those enemies that tried to bring me down
Your composure is significant
So please refrain from wearing a frown
Let green peace allow this
Boxed world to freely exit their cages
Those acting as superior
Occasionally guide and lead the stages
Stages of the play
Stages of successions in a world that you own
Comprehending all of this
You sing in a self soothing tone
The heavens
Cling to number sevens
Finding faith I now do cling
Clairvoyant images and visions
The select few comfortably are able to bring

PARABLES AND PROBLEMS

Read the writing on the wall
Observe the treasures of those
Fortunate souls down the hall
Paranoid beliefs are mine to own
All seeds were planted
Yet to my amazement nothing was sown
This grieving ordeal that I witness
Is burdening me
And bringing me deep down
Misunderstood scapegoat chased away
I am the talk of the town
I thought my enemies
Might grow to respect or love me
The doors are locked
And I am without God's numbers predestined key
I realize now that frustration
Is a pill that I eat
Yet not too swallow
Transparency drawn within itself
Cornered now and my senses feeling hallow
Society has pushed
Yet I still did not fall
I begin to run
As you just did waddle and crawl
This logic that I supply
Is from an overabundance
Of my back against the ropes
Futility denies
Both near and distant hopes
The light at the end
Of the tunnel burns
The freight train chugs
As the engine churns
Winners sometimes quit
And losers sometimes win
But tycoons and tyrants
See this as the cardinal sin
These stories I tell you
Shine some radiance
Of divine glow
Or just a trifling thought
That somehow my friend the
Yesterdays have fundamentally taught

PLEASE DON'T FORGET

Forgotten things are remembered
I see that my love for you
Never will meet it's demise
I still value our passionate love
And am benevolent at the size
The coin was flipped
And the ante of jackpot was set
Living with or without you
Convinced nobody will win the bet
Dreams of you were shared alike
Becoming that of an infinite quest
I gave my love
And you gave me the best
I read a letter that you sent
It is quite weathered
The pages being soiled, ruffled, and bent
Nice to have seen your pictures
And the writings that are noble.
My search for a love like this
Is geographically far
The moon does glisten
And you are that star
The years do compile
Time uniquely though shows no remorse
Sentiments of my Creator
To keep me on course
I will speak for myself
And let my actions speak to my friends
Life being a militaristic strategy
And goes globally to all ends
I pray for you
From time to time
Whistling your tune
And playing hop scotch with the rhyme
Dear lover
Please forever touch my heart
Dear lover
Without you no way to restart
Sometimes caught amongst my confusions
I pray for the phone to ring
Yet I'm comforted with your voice
Becoming bewildered
A party to reunite and ecstatically rejoice
The pages are turning
And the narrator being my inner voice
Please forgive me
I'll forgive you
We are torn apart
And not sticking like glue
Yet morning does arrive
As insomnia this night has kept me alive
Complex very intricate emotions
Although apart our relationship will survive
We will be together again

Or at least I think
Vertigo sets in
Alcohol pleads desperate for me to drink
We will be again
Again we will be
God on our side
Joy forever to see
I will be with you soon
In this world and the next
I'll conclude my diary now
And let our future possibilities be the text

Propelling the Senses

My senses appear as if to be propelled
Be it force or impulse
Inner logic with it's twist has compelled
Total awareness has derived allowing decisions
For my conscious to be much more alert
Combating against angst
As though soldiers guarding annealed against hurt
Termination
Rid myself of these memories of enemies
And their trudging path of war
Do not turn your back for much too long
For ambushed attack leaves me fighting intense as the core
Devise a heroic plan
Strategy a must
Oblivious to crooked behind the scenes favors and such
God my only friend ultimately whom I do trust
Have you ever read into Liturgics
Will this bestowed intervention calm what is corrupt
A tainted world running
An earthquake contained appears that it will not erupt
Will my prayers be answered
And will they be heard
Scripture indicates fulfillment instilled with it's holy word
Do you ever truly ever recover from an ongoing barrage
Distorted blurs of reality
Resemble that of a mirage
Am I seeing things
Do my senses demonstrate legitimate worth
Does even e.s.p. have it's divisions
And was I part of the equation my name spelled at birth
Miscreant
Antecedent
Why was I this recipient
Your conduct is far from lawful
An audience awaits a barren sheep to be jeered
Forked tongues cut as a blade
And blatantly the rivals have sheered
When spiritual war finds you
And I promise that it will
Do not fall prey to the oppressors
And allow for the vicious thrill
Suffering
A ship at vicious sea yet drowning without sails
Clinging to life finding hope Is comforted by heavenly favor
Alone I lay upon this bed prodded with nails
With the thoughts of home I begin to savor
Inspiration or survival
Just what is driving me around this maze
Frantically I ask for directions
And almost senseless lethargically the explainer just delays

PROPHECY REVEALED

Quit feeding the poison
And open the holy books
Were you included
If so who is the perpetrating crooks
Prophecies of the divine saint
Overwhelming propaganda
But please do not faint
Predicting a new religion and safety
Of all of those alive
Opposite of end times
We all shall survive
Morality and oneness
Equal complacency of fact
A method of simple joy
Keeps everything justifiably intact
The movement is small
But the mission is so much
When objects turn to gold
Upon just a hand's touch
Put the salve on the cut
Everything is possible
Direction finds itself pulled away from the rut
Though conflicting is our sight
Choices hopefully become decisions
And are vested by that right
Hands in prayer
So much time spent
Resorting to the maker above
Faith in action
Is determined only by love
Perpetual motion
Life climbs and descends
Such as a roller coaster on wheels
See the soldiers downtrodden
Yet they dig in their heels
We are one of the same
And same of the one
A sanctimonious expanse
Lead's us to God's holy son

PUBLIC EYE

At times it appears seemingly nothing more than an
Ongoing yet sickening and menacing media blitz
Flogging is at it's threshold and local subversive
Tyrants just can't resist to get in their hits
Concoctions of distorted views with outlandish stories to tell
I can see how even temporal escapes still have abundant fits
Fits of rage
Fits of joy
Fits to the devoted
Engaged into success
Not seeing money necessarily as their personal toy
But that is the persona or truth believed
If that was the main focus how could I have achieved
A give and take
A take and give
Proponents or merely fashioned essentials
That equate to now I may moderately live
Contents fragile as a figure of speech so handle with care
Being star struck along with it's qualities can be great
Say what you want....that is if you so dare
Maybe my thinking is less systematic and relates to that of old
Never did I claim to be an expert
Maybe my lack of logic looks inward and readily should scold
Euphemistically
A fool like me restrained sometimes does sugar coat
Statistically
We are all our own individual watch me again miss the boat
Public eye
Does the Paparazzi hound you ravenously
Even if you throw them a bone
They will devour with contentment anxiously
And scare you possibly to pieces and strewn from the throne
Public eye
Have your dreams been fulfilled
This is all worth it though
As you will find not truly chasing your dreams is pseudo impressions
Of the mind and that the twist finds it is also foe
High
Not feeling low
The morning awakens you and is bellowed in by the black crow
The stars in this world have ability to
Communicate to a world that is precious and near
People yet not nature sometimes duplicitous and evolving
And on this sphere rotate around a strange hemisphere
Wherever and whoever you are in life please remember this
The price of victory is not accountable financially
So accomplish and hopefully one day you won't regret or miss

QUESTIONS OF LOYALTY

Within others
We all seek to find trust
The volcano fire spoils
And spews earthly crust
My blood boils
As I excessively see red
Unlucky partnerships result
Being slight fear enticed with dread
Do what you say
Say what you do
A missing link
Mystery conceals the hidden shoe
Allowing exceptions according
To every rule
Compiling upon vulnerability
Traces of a troublemaker who defiantly quit school
Read these words
Understand what they mean
Obviously a material universe
Is also transposed into the Almighty green
Decision
Agreement based upon choice
Suspicion
Questions do arouse cordially from outward voice
Not needing the highlife
Is modesty within hands clasp
Falling from the cliff
With nothing to grasp
Faithful
Both to a cause
Possibly reconciling with amend
People and places
Deservingly will commend
Trust and loyalty
Specialize in frank and honest action
Chemistry
Find what works for others
Chip away
With what just does work
Analyze
Do all the parts fit
Subside
Principles equating to sustain or quit
Sovereignty
Politics of person
Or simply being empowered
Step to the plate
And see the pitcher as the coward
Juggle the dimensions
Of balance and a souls worth
Explore the depths of kindness
Give praise to this merciful birth
Loyalty is pursuit of trust
Keep purity
From decaying within smothering rust

REALLY QUITE FAR FROM ABSURD

Do not call this absurd
Divine words redeem radiating mercy
Interesting as I see this as holy word
Holy word
Converted thought
Bids to be free of sin and guilt and sin
Onward this valiant struggle has been fought
Three crosses
Only one nailed and hailed as the King of Jews
Bad word spreads faster than good
Yet surfacing with Noah's flood whose to hear the news
Mankind's sins burdened upon Christ via the bloodied cross
Calvary itself being the agonizing test
Nailed to a cross yet without his father's desertion
Drained slowly of life
Now nearly deplete of mental and physical exertion
Solid communication
See the paid price on the cross a cure
A creation marked though with it's own rules
The false past pretenses speed becoming that of a blur
Convincing and alleviating
Pray for comfort along all of your days
An earnest host is unique and gifted
And may be cordial enough to give forthright praise
Purged
Submerged
Cleansed while baptism atones
Feeding this spirit and soul
My stomach pangs for food and desperately it moans
Abiding necessary steps to sanctify
I am reading your mind
Yet I do not know the reason why
Redeem
Go to the extreme
Tonic tranquil thoughts pacify a material world
Leek thoughts diffusing allowing me to see my dream
Yet I am different
My difference may just be lack of voice
An internal establishment conveying intentions that yearn
Listen as my hearts thundering beats with rejoice
Are you an outsider
Yet not mocking faith such as an iconoclast
Disbeliefs of your personifications
Within itself an identity always seems to last
A subtle voice speaks form the outside in
A resplendent tongue blurts words nearly audible
Camouflaged now beneath what becomes chagrin
In notion take this with a grain of salt
Realizing that your integrity was under attack
Yet returning with a smile as result

REVIEWING MY PRAYER CARD

You prayed for me
I prayed for answers
And my prayers became answered
In a dizzying blur
The solutions are real
That much I am sure
Visions of a happier land
Come to my brain
One with more comfort
And minimal being the pain
There is no bloodshed
No wars did I see
Just human life that was
Docile and completely free
But this story your hearing
I am not quite sure
How it came about
Blossoming seeds flourish as beauty
And quickly they sprout
Count your blessings
Give divine inspiration a budge
You may be your worst critic
Yet not your soul's judge
Pray that modern medicine
Will soon find a cure for all diseased
Because millions are stricken
And in prayer are found on bended knees
Sin plagues the human soul
Playing warden to a destitute source
Inner drive increases
As I sense an omni-potent source
As servants of the Lord
We see the world in a different light
Graciously giving to brothers and sisters
Even when resources are tight
Be thankful for what you have
And what is naught
Observing the today
And understanding what was taught
Scrupulously taking a stand
Against right and wrong
Undiscriminating my prayers are definitely conceded
To my higher power above
Focus upon others
Ultimate adherence to love
Prayers are derived from God's time table
And not of our own
Understanding this gift
Within myself I have grown

Spiritual Citizenship

So I have all of these brilliant credentials now
Construed beginnings I believe equal to total winnings
At current I feel as if I have complete choice and choose as though a cow
Chomp, chomp, grind, grind, chew, choose
Follow this rendition along with its interesting parable
And I speculate my true friend of longevity that you just cannot and will not lose
Just what in your life anchors you down with or within risk
Actually now ostracizing is real and it is about the pain that I am able to internally feel
Look within for what you have to remedy this discord of action and find ultimately satisfaction
Now you know that you have that force of spiritualism and it is for real
An overwhelming taste and desire for success and the holy word
The choice for you then is unequaled as zeal
Apparently then-I am human
Such as you
Guiding these hands upon a rubic's cube
Yet it is only solvable by us two
Creating church or so to say sanctum
Where
Wherever you are at
Silence the dominant vain viper
You can still obtain millions and not behave as an adult brat
Love both God and his son Jesus Christ
Because as a believer that is the main focus of where it is at
Christ died for all of us and our inevitable sins
Which perpetuates as humanity proceeds forthright
And only glorifies itself within victories and signifies as only contented wins
So keep this in mind
And may I add to this word that you never forget
To silence the beast and in effort to win this ongoing war
Stifle and baffle with prayer and faith in action to cause your enemies regret
Prayer chains in the name of Almighty God to say the least
An everyday gathering of believers is culminating
As there is now a meal that is communed with and for a Thanksgiving like feast
Do you know of the ultimate burden and transgression that God's son did carry
It earned him the cross of salvation yet he was known by most as the High Priest
Believe
In yours and you
Relieve
And the joy of life just seems to shine through
Achieve
Action, word, deed and even yes your highest goal
Conceive
And one day your wife shall exhibit your lives roll
Drive
Never stop pushing forward in vigor
Stay alive
For everyday is a gift
Thrift
A penny saved is….well….a penny!
Swift
A cunning mind will not fall behind if exercised complete
Equipped
For the ultimate desire of humans instilled should be to acquire a heavenly seat

This is my mini plan to live a spiritual life and how to have fun!
If you get confused read in sunshine's free gift adorned by the warm sun!

SPOKEN WORD

Words of spoken tenacity
Are being spoken from a gingerly start
Yet I ask of what do I pertain
So much that I need to get off my heart
Very much I need to explain
Dreams
Am I within the power of persuasion
To show you just what my love does offer
Hypothetically
True emotions perplexing with people of plastic
Analytically
Conclusions drawn that I don't fit in the clique
What will keep me at the norm
My mind is it's own worst enemy
And it seems like brain surgery I should immediately perform
Yet both equate to prove a pondering point
Rapidly losing my faith with supposed Christians
Would God kindly reconcile and anoint
And speak from a heart of virtue
Being shed and kicked down
Show me the light so that I may get thru
Some so greatly granted
Yet some got so cheated
Playing this game without all of the pieces
How so could I have successfully competed
Fate of God at times seems to poison my once sweet
Passion of freewill and chance
Is it still God's angels I follow
I hear the screaming inner voice and take my stance
God can do anything
100 times faster than we can blink our eye
I am listening to find
While we are all in the grind
I must look deep to keep you in mind
I attempt to see the brighter other sides inflection
Open doors
Opportunities coming to you all direction
Not allowing for oppression other's imposed doubt
Feeding the hungry soul at any detection
Look within
For you have so much to offer and give
Life congruent with it's unique experiences
The ultimate answer although is to cordially live
Become familiar with a higher power
Past mistakes hopefully are seen as stepping stones
And henceforth strength meets euphoria which just won't cower
Examine your past
Yet look to the future to see a brighter tomorrow
Stay in touch with emotional amplitude
And gracefully understand this as graceful sorrow
We have been given a unique gift
One that is respondent not with want yet needs
The battle is defined by the relentless yet swift
When the world knocks you down

Get back up and fight twice as hard again
Because even those who were once lost
Find triumphantly ways to earn a win
Lost still within which side although to pick
Is not always so fun
Worries could overwhelm you and as your body stays still
The innocent mind is on the run

SWEET VALOR

Ignorance or neglect
Inside of which medium
Do these adversaries seem to reflect
If I add my add cents up
Will you either accept or object
Your actions are determinable with prediction
Yet with you conveying this message
To the masses it attributes to its own restriction
Do you know although what I mean
Do you see what I say
Often times the sum of disgruntling lawyer logic dismay
If we are to win this war
We first must win over ourselves
For this war being sold unfortunately is insurmountable
And is being stockpiled with wounded lives on the shelves
Can we end this war and just who is held accountable
Sweet valor
What is the recipe spewed out of a canteen
Invigorating and hard to handle
Yet no metaphors to show what I mean
Just cool H20
An M.R.E. for tonight's meal
I look to my chain of commands and higher ups
To stay positive and form a reaction of platoon zeal
My senses seem magnified this twilight night
And even though hardened I can emotionally feel
I close my eyes as my closed eyes now seem
To find me within my spirited mind
Pictures and memories now return along with my
Last letter that I now remember being joyfully signed
I miss you all so much
I can't even begin to explain
I need something to soothe
And from the east comes a soft trickling rain
Conversations with other soldiers give and boost the morale
I know that maybe peace is profitable
Yet it seems like no one wants to cash in on the sale
In a situation of war
Once the bloodshed is all counted did anyone gain victory
It's hard to say
But I can hear the beg for peace and understand the plea
As a soldier
I will entrust with you to stay utmost benevolent
Yet even though all senses strong
Gain comfort in your acceptance as a warrior
And no longer a worrier

TEACH ME TO LOVE

We have all experienced
Our fair share of hate
Reconciliation answers to Godly forgiveness
Don't give up it is not too late
Yet no one understands
This territory of disregard
A setback chronologically in time
I feel as if I
Have been both feathered and tarred
I need somebody to
Show me how to love again
People burst my fragile bubble
And appallingly laugh as
They hold the pin
I fight tooth and nail for
The little that I own
Others plant my seed
Yet nothing except infinite
Grimness was what was sown
A few go
Through life misunderstood
Bouncing along the doors
Like a pinball trapped
In an obstacle electrical maze
Yet for only a quarter
Check your coordinated ways
Watch the dart fly
As the dartboard does await
Nothing but bulls-eyes
Isn't this great
What is recondite and obscure
Behind hidden eyes
Is a snapshot of calamity
Or as I see it
I would further to call it exonerated depravity
Some days I wish would never end
Temporary spiritual bliss
Yet is this the way to mend
I aim to correct myself
Yet never underestimate my belief
Love can't be seen
But it's actions are observed
Missionary of this world's contentment
Because even the unfaithful smugly have served
Loneliness can be an immovable weight
A toddler with etch-a -scetch
Shall attempt to erase as new the slate

THE FINE ART OF FORGIVENESS

I have heard now the news that you have been tremendously hurt
Although not literally
It appears as if that you have been wrongly treated as if dirt
Understand I do feel your pain
And yes I have been there before
The hurt quite evident
And you feel as though you are trapped within a revolving door
Never did you plan on this
Never knowing of these things
Who would ever calculate or imagine this stuff was in store
But it is time to make a 180 degree change
At this exact moment my friend you should
Snatch your assailer and with his or her motives make a true exchange
Voice yourself and let them know that you are human
They and them the same as yourself
And knowing this fact
You collect memory books and do not like what they forced upon your shelf
Be understanding yet strangely enough slow to modification
This will employ that you and yours
Will not only get through but enjoy their numbered days duration
Each exact answer of forgiveness is difficult I am sure
Yet once established and then carried out
The benefit and reward is Utopian and creates a heartfelt cure
There is I believe possibly no exact order in how to forgive
Yet if you manage to connect with Christ to speak to God
The answer will be salvation with forgiveness
Allowing for both to once again diligently live
But you exclaim that you were extremely hurt
But your big heart fashions itself although and definitely cares
For the one that savagely hurt you
As you look to the heavens you can see them widening
And your vision allows a way to see it thru
Back to your mission
For I know that you will not back down
Even if stifled
You will throw off your enemies
And obscure them with a right side up inverted frown
Good beit there will not be division
I suspect that if you even somewhat follow this plan
Prayer alone will guide you
And intuition through channeled direction will service
And find its home to perpetually see you thru
God is love
Knowing this understand that we are all created in Gods image
Take this to heart
Then sadly enough even if you were to lose it all
The beginning is easier-All that much more wisdom just back to the start
Forgiving finds the stronger one
Empty handed and penniless pockets goes often those in those
Whose belief was often times short
If this statement is false
Please forgive me and just reply with a word of retort
I hope that you feel better

I genuinely say that I do
Because within us all is a space pleading for love
And ultimately it is God who is doing the planting
It is up to us knowing just what to do

THE TRAP IS SET

Manipulation
A method which the opponent does use
Abuse Refuse
Blood in my veins
The catalyst substance that you transfuse
Insidious
Oblivious
This creation of yours
You mold by hand
The putty substance being firmly pliable
Much different than sand
Despite the intense madness
A deranged scientist
Does not necessarily find a cure
A strange deep fantasy possibly fulfilled
Yet looking back even skepticism is not sure
The intrigue of the obscure
Equates to what mainstream fashions
And the meek must endure
The sin of human touch
Malice or magic
Entwines the spiders web
A victims fate is untimely and tragic
Within this game of life
Adherence to remaining I contain and clench
A loyal friend and acquaintance
I'm always there in a pinch
I have run and I have hid
Such as an existent cockroach
Nearly impossible to terminate or rid
Was Darwin right
That only the strong survive
This philosophy or doctrine encompassed
Perfection within the meaning of contrive
Rat Poisons snare has been scattered
The awaiting plebian rats soon shall eat
A superficial capture
Is far from being a courageous feat
Can't you see
Either thru ambition or instinct
I am headstrong
Promising not to fall to the enemy
I sing my victory song
The crosshairs zero in
On someone or something
What or who is in sight
Night vision goggles not needed
Regardless that it is a dark black night
When ambushed
Combat with what you must
Staying alive with common reason
Is my mortifying lust
If you comply with these
Words another eventful day is nearing

Dawns brilliant sunlight is drawing close
There is no need to be awkward or fearing
A lesson in overcoming lives tests
Becoming free at all costs
That much I have confidently confessed

THE PAGE THAT WAS TORN OUT

The pages inwardly turn
My soul deepens
All emphasis contained now within learn
Longing to live
And giving so much
Just to try
Superimposed circumstance
Trapped I see a self contained picture within your eye
Strangely the picture that I see
Is formulated both
From past and present
Steadfast ascent and flagrant descent
What comes second nature to some
Grossly spoils to the unfortunate
Malignancy of the diseased bum
Try and try again
Those who do not
Compromise only with fiendish sin
Verdicts of self judgment
Allocate the loss while forgetting how to win
Does either aptitude or ability
Understand this confusion
Does this book have a page torn out
Manifesting itself as obloquy or illusion
Deism
Is this book of hopes with spiritualism complete
Pastors of the new world
Have arms wide open and do anxiously greet
The tonic of life
As invigorating as it may seem
Is accomplishment of hopes
Or shall we say a wide awake dream
Will I get there
How far away is it for me
Beauty of attraction
Allows for subtly of the partial eclipse to even see
I sometimes have been that sun
Obscured by that moon
Feeling out of sorts
Comedies satire finds me as the buffoon
I am in search
For my missing page
In your book
Do you have a page missing too
Shockingly enough no seeds were planted
Yet still your garden thrived as it grew
Indecision
Revision
Freewill allows for change
Innermost mind calculations
To keep from what could derange
Extraction
Refraction
The bending of light lays

I am completely alert
Yet maybe you should disregard this because I am in a daze
Question or merely examples
Just what is your remark

TRANSLATED TENACIOUSNESS

I took a walk today
As my brain entertained
My vivid imagination
I wandered cross this world
All over God's aggrandized creation
Perplexed although certainly- I felt delusion
Are my thoughts owned by me or just an illusion
I contemplated what is real
And just what acts as colossal confusion
My senses appear sound
But as for explanation
Direction does not seem so profound
Tangled nagging questions
Overtly come to my mind
If the yesterdays were so great
Could I put this life in rewind
Continually thoughts of futures uncertainty
Unfold for me to mentally view
Is it true
life not a marked slate
A fresh day wakens us as new
Or is it scheming
That accounts for menacing nightmares
Or visions that were pleasantly dreamed
What is perceived is sometimes
Only what is believed
Tangible proof is typically what separates
Fact from fiction
What is your belief
Or does faith speak in contradiction
Bad news travels faster
Than the good
Uniquely trivial
And completely misunderstood
Trust begins to grow weaker
Inner voices whispering
Yet I cannot determine who is the speaker
I try to see an open door
As a new opportunity
Something with which there is much in store
Yet many may slam or shut
I won't let my sincere efforts
Fall into a rut
Mother earth draws pictures
An audience of billions
Records everything and writes
Their own books
Do not allow shallow minds to steal
For they might devour your dreams
And as a banana they eat while they peel

TRICKS OF TIME

Tick tock
Tick tock
Apparently so
Once life is conceived
Time never does end
Begging for harmony
With rationalization readily to lend
Pain
Sometimes a second
Appears to be an hour
A marionette on strings
Exhibiting loss of self power
Time
It does not wait on us
Because forward it does march
A unique recipe to win through effort
With daily bread derived from starch
Although restricted
I allow my action to speak
Louder than word
Calculate your dream
Now a friend of the absurd
To God
A month may seem a day
Adults on recess
Today the assignment is to play
Leisure
A method to pacify
And ultimately to persevere
Check your watch
Because the time is near
Until that time
Work propaganda at hand
And embrace the toil
Flowers originate from earthly top soil
Petition your brain
Please acknowledge the plea
Hang in there
Soon you will be free
Free to plan
Free to choose
Yet just what or who
Factors into win or lose
Determination
Hopes to always succeed
Procrastination
The antagonist of need
Find a guide
When there is no compass to follow
Spiritual awakening
Shines both sacred as it does hallow

TRUST WITHIN ME

Your emotions are revealed
By and according to your prolonged inner voice
Contemplation observes what is deemed as right
Basis definitive only upon choice
Fleeing from the obvious yet what seems right
Existence or onward success
Weak minds approach what is definitively strong
Trusting within myself
Not quite sure of a strangers hand
Unlock yourself from this gripping hold
Decaying bread
Is rancid , nasty, and smothered in mold
Honesty conveyed
The conscience only what has told
I cannot remember my ego
Ever being so jubilant and thrilled
The bloodied knives you quickly
Must pull from your back
Betrayers and liars
Symbolize possibly intentionally those who lack
Gold mines; Fort Knox
Banks filled to the seams
Do not necessarily equate
To the purpose of everybody's dreams
Loyal friend
Clench my outstretched hand
That renders guidance and hope
Cleansing the souls impurities
The tub bathes in water and soap
Gaining and acquiring
Friendships of commendable worth
Develop from within your heart
Life not always a sweet treat
The taste of remedy strangely can also be somehow tart
Visualize; captivate
Always now
Therefore never late
Is there a price to be set
What is the ante set at
What is the purse
The pressure is on big time
Within the house is there a nurse
Is there a cure
Focus upon solid foundation
Eliminates confusions trap and targets the unsure
Rules to a game
Begin to set and formulate
Maybe we should take a spiritual consensus
All bodily senses fulfilled as if high
Acknowledging utopia and dialoguing bliss
A friend of myself
A friend of yours
Oceans of deep seeded interest
Readily locating the seashores

TWISTED TOTAL AWARENESS

Total awareness
Ultimately finds itself nestled and concurring
With both sweat and dispositional tears
You have to bite the bullet
Release those aggravating fears
Marching forward as if in
An abstract game of charades
Belittled and becoming the clown
Humiliatingly being displayed in local parades
Just when to obstinate
Yes it has found a home in me
Refusing to lose this fight
Pushing to the accelerated top
And vigorous is the might
Out of body experience
My mind is alert
Yet my cold body is numb
Tangled become my senses
Melodrama entwines what is different and glum
Intricately the web is sown
Innumerable are lives trials
That much is known
Tribulations surface to all
Whispers of misunderstandings
Hoping these inner demons fall
Innocence
Sheds it's light and qualities
Of inner peace and calmness
Efforts to break loose from the harness
Being a spectator to my own
Life creates pervading curiosity
The universe makes prey of the weak
Tongue tied allegations
Transformations that plainly do speak
Pitiless mirrors laughing at me
As if in a dare
Firmly I stand poker-faced though
Throughout this untimely agonizing stare
Not a delusion
A concrete tangible situation
Scoring up a factor of obloquy
Taunting and heckling me
With evil perverse words to say
What the conscience hides
From the soul although is actually quite a lot
Unnervingly the mind maybe plays tricks
Fashionably false and disingenuous
Although some pseudo betrayers hide behind their crucifix

WRITTEN BY : BRIAN MOILANEN

VEXATIOUS

I came to this world
Apparently in a normal way
Compilations of experiences
Yet burdened with should I stay or leave
Precociousness follows
A grasp that isn't always though easy to achieve
Insurmountably ineptness does surface
And never wants to depart
It's all within the game
And leaves behind a broken heart
Maybe difficulty lies in
Building bonding valuable partnerships
Yet wars are waged
And the scale of balance tips
What friends to keep
Which ones own up to being loyal
Reading manuscripts of human life
Amidst the maddening turmoil
Telepathy
Crystal ball
Untold future
Natures call
Some will climb
Yet others fall
Creeping up behind my own shadows
And feeling very small
Yet continually in pursuit of truth
The dim light still shines
And gives this soul a chance to renew
Without a single trouble
Just where would we be
Heaven on earth
That's what would inhibit what we would see
Yet troubles linger
Unhesitatingly we attempt
To sweep them under the rug
An anecdotal cure
Maybe a unique divine drug
Something to guide
Something to coax
Something to remedy
And break any possible hoax
Humbling myself
I realize only my troubles
Am I understandably able to solve
I don't believe in hocus- pocus
God speaks thru and with others
To solve our problems in
An earnest regard
Cutting through the sweet butter
Yet our problems are sickening as lard
Never give up the fight
Punch until happiness begins
Let us see if our Maker is true
And forgives us of our confessed sins

WHAT IS BEYOND

The time has now come
Predicting the future
And intoxicated with rum
Constellations and scheming
Keep the astrological sane
See your horoscope fashion itself as
An illustrator and design it's reign
Consequently to belief
Other worlds with life seem a relief
People paint the earth
And also the earth paints people
Tight rope walking
Upon the church steeple
Science and frontiers
The possibility of more
Keep your sights open
Only to pay reverence for what is in store
Man walked on the moon
Other planets
Entertain the realms soon
A million worlds
Black holes and such
Almost inconceivable
Yet intrigued with indescribable touch
Mankind beginning to understand
That a hungry world
Is in a tempering demand
Products of infinity
Are in the skies to observe
And this land sometimes penitently questions
Yet it is science they serve
A rubic's cube for
Humans to solve
The mind is wandering
Eloquently did we evolve
Where did the dinosaurs come from
Aliens might laugh
At an inferior being
My mind is open
It just won't close
I am real
It's you that should drop the pose

WHAT SHOULD I DO

What should I do
Now that you are gone
Playing chess with only a few of the pieces
No way to again capture your pawn
I really really do miss you
Now and through the never ending tomorrow
I camouflage my tears
Yet you can still see my hidden sorrow
I am not surprised if this melancholy results
In stares and unkind jeers
Our love was interesting with every detail unique
Now frustrated and at a lonely loss
I cannot find proper words to plainly speak
My fractured soul is in definite need of repair
Turn a nightmare back to fantasy
Deciphering with ability to remove the scare
Our time spent together
Was always filled with a celestial glow
No longer casually fishing together at the pond
And visionaries alike getting caught amongst the undertow
Pictures of you clutter the bedroom floor
Sailing away are sweet memories
A sea with no surrounding shore
A kid with a nickel
Inside a pristine candy store
Photographs
Paintings
Letters that you wrote
This preserves those good times
And I see this as our infinite antidote
Yet if you can still find me
Can you truly find yourself
Because just who is the investor
Of these quality years upon the shelf
Time
Do not spend too much of it yesteryear
For this might paradox itself in situations
Culminating only as either joy or fear
My wings may have been clipped
But somehow I still do fly
Am I too late for this continued love
Does the situation seem nigh
Nearly impossible I remain compelled
Fighting off resistance I can't hear
All the negatives that you have yelled
I think being docile favors the intimate
While the upper hand may just be given to the poor
An unlimited supply of money
With time to spend in a department store
Where are you now
In this never ending maze of life
Doing battle within your own mind
These sick calculations being methods of strife

WHAT WILL BECOME

The marvel brain develops
And forwardly the
impulsive conscious envelopes
What will remarkably become of everything
Watch the days become garish with the Almighty's sword
Onward I cry for my girl which beckons me to sing
The ability to use my mental and physical exertion
Which serves as a guide amongst both obstacle and empire
Scorned goes the penniless prophet bewildered without employment
Without doubt his sacrifices will find him to be hired
Stay positive in a world of insincere absolution
Add it up and do the math
I see this as possibly prescribed restitution
Glamour
Justice's Hammer
People who stammer
I see myself often times falling in love
Yet still not quite sure of my suspicion of you
Remember
This sticky substance is now infinite and forms as glue
Don't pretend
Take time to lend
Is thinking in itself what does apprehend
Outstanding
Distinguished at always a cathartic marvel
Safety equals only to prominence
Sunshine lights fun this day at the local carnival
Poker
Fate, Free will, Strategy unique
Sometimes just what contributes to a win
Qualities pondering with soft voice to speak
Think about it and ponder
Your brain being knotty with thought tranquil
Decency and material only tangible therefore concrete
Only on the chess board in which you should kill
Reverence
Even the meek in a troubled world are rewarded with some
The ants also must survive
And also for them the bread of life is alive
The necessity of pleasure implicates the wonder of fun
It is not right or wrong just the ability to use voice
Some are confused
Others are abused
Victimization
I have felt it burdened upon me like a ton of bricks
Victory
Slight of hand or ultimate magic unveils mysterious tricks
Putting the gamut of feelings in the blender
Placing all bets my life and experiences will equate someday to glee
At the current moment I miss you
And memories enough just do not fill this void
Frustration finds itself venting quietly alone
An observable transformation torn being angry and annoyed
Love

Compassion filled with kiss
Intimacy finds itself aroused with a touch of sensuality
Right now I am complete and efficaciously effervescent
My state of being normal
I now see the future as beyond more than a beyond present

When I was young

A library full of exciting memories
A collection of maundering or strangely
enough sophisticated thoughts
Words and action oriented deeds
Staying banausic in my adult years
Supplying some wants
And accomplishing all needs
Past recollections now come
To tangible view
Moods and emotions are
Illustrated within these photographs
Bad hair days
A parody of laughs
A choice to become
Better or bitter
The Christmas tree glows
And is decorated with glitter
When I was a kid
I thought I
Knew it all
A black eye some Friday night
Resulting from a bar room brawl
Times marching forward
I recall my first class
Grade of an A
A loss for words
What to do and what to say
No longer a kid
Now I have kids of my own
Now in high rank
I sit upon my adorned throne
My princess
May I call her my sweetening wife
Sees our long time together
As a mutual complete life
Managing to locate letters
From old chums
A feast for all
Not just a plate of crumbs
That is what I remember them for
A winning chance for everyone
Opportunities knocking door
That is what I prescribe
Calculations translated and recorded
An item in which to transcribe
Now I am quite old
Yet in delicate transmission
Understand that my story was told
And wonder if you love me as my only suspicion

WINGS OBTAINED

I see the purged coloring rainbow
And expect at it's end
To find the pot of gold
I have waited forever
And will not grow old
The hands of time
Have abruptly come to a halt
Answers to untimely prayers
Becoming the precious result
I am now in heaven
The pie in the sky
That I craved
Where I now know
I am cherished conceding as eternally saved
No longer engaged into fight
Ascending wings carry me
An angel off in flight
Now set apart for my divine purpose
Coded divine rules to follow
My altered conscience begins to rehearse
God is graciously kind
The kingdoms streets paved with gold
Living Bible chapters
Now before me begin to unfold
No more pain
No tears shed
Here light always shines
Therefore the need regards for any bed
Dreams now are reality
Nothing at all to dread
Now belonging to the highest
Superior beings known in the galaxies
Desperate apologetic sinners
Redemptions brilliance delivers to appease
What you perceived as
A cloud in the air
Was my white robed winged body
All eyes watching plot loves care
I understand and see
Your saddened remorse
Credentials of intellectual understanding
Keep me on course
Intimacy glorifies its role
A sense of care grants well being
Empowerment given freely from our praised God
Slavery's grip is fleeing
Break the slate
Remold the concrete
Freewill' s choice
Appears limitless and complete
Behind I leave only joy
Which is to give
Also here is my childhoods toy
Time passing allows to forget

Goodbye for now
One day I will see you soon
Tabernacles choir of angels
Is playing your favorite tune

WITH WHICH TO PONDER

Don't be so quick to reveal
Obscurity of the extraordinary senses
An odd while yet unique enchanting feel
The doors of heaven
Now are wide open
For all in the world to see
Or to the naysayer a figment of imagination
Uttering a subtle whisper of leave me be
Come as you are
Not necessarily what you should become
Inspiring words to encourage those deemed sociably insignificant
Agnostic, illiterate or dumb
Think and ponder with because
Some stern words say just too much
Difficult to understand
Yet intrigued with love and genuine touch
Don't let the rivers run dry
Tears forming these here waters
Are being exhibited from your cry
Don't be mislead
Both at times these waters and land are fierce
So lightly please do tread
Contentment helps me find
Somehow a place within this absurdity
I know that others may have desire for riches
And yes they may apparently temporarily heal as desired plea
Without even the analgesic need for stitches
But my inner drive seeks more than that
They may fall prey
Within the trap previously set to catch the rat
Emotions may rise in doing so
Honesty may yet but should not fall
Yet we learn as we go
What is self intuition
Is this the same as natures call
What makes us tick
The inner clocks
Are they wound -time thru an hourglass
With minimal noise being the utter miniscule sound
Yet there is sound and that is good
For those with which to ponder often go unheard
And unfortunately partner- misunderstood

You have already won

Beauty is characterized by
The inside and not the out
Exempt of wealth and riches
Yet still displaying humbling clout
Winners display exigency
To others welfares
And not always to their own
Demands of retributions and equality
Understanding forthright that we have no clone
What determines a winner is subjective
To say the least
Difficulties for everyone
Claims the righteous priest
A winner is not based on
What you have
It's based upon having
What you gave
Being free on this occasionally hoisted earth
And not living dejected and being a hardened slave
Not that it has too be tangible gifts
A loving hug
Or a destined kiss
Not being with loved ones
Now that is the closeness that I miss
A family of friends
Now these friends form a family
Brothers and sisters unite
Straying from wickedness
I know this is within our sight
Becoming a better person
Horrified by eternal burn
Peddling up a never ending hill
As the wheels do turn
A complete revolution of
Human bodies attached to a fixed path
Problems and solutions
Glorifications reckon to spoil the wrath
Turning from the devil
Not allowing myself to fall in the bottomless pit
Lives of actions and deeds
The sun is which my world does orbit
Lessons in love
The elderly might be able to explain
Their radiance that of a horoscope
Predictable yet very far from being inane
A temporary heaven
Occasionally finds us on earth
Remind yourself always
That all life has its potential and purport of worth

CREDITS

Wow....Just where to begin and just where to end. This sounds very cliché if you will, but it is exactly where I am at this given moment to be quite honest! I want to I suspect, begin by saying I want to begin by thanking God Almighty who has given me the drive, strive, admiration, ideas, inspiration and perseverance, ultimately for writing this here book. Wow....o.k. Now to thank a lot of other reputable persons. My mom and dad. Their formal names being Kenneth And Victoria Moilanen. They would always lend an ear when I had a new, or old poem, to offer their way!

Thanks, you helped my alter ego, so to say! Seriously, and also thanks for the tidbits of advice, dad. It helped. You da' man! I want to next thank my sister Michelle, who also listened to a lot of my ideas and also to many of my poems. Thanks! I have certainly appreciated all of your input.

I would also like thank my nephew Taylor Anderson, who enlightened me with inspiration of Christianity and team prayer for team sports for his High School. Way cool, kid! He is a studious hard worker with great grades and not to mention a great athlete! Thumbs up, champ! Next up on the thank-you list is Dr. Jerry Csokasy who has always offered great advice and certainly has been a whirlwind of successful upbeat positive talk to keep me striving on that road of revision. Thanks, Dr. Jerry. You are so inspiring and help so many people. Much appreciation. Next up is Genesis Clubhouse, thanks to both staff and clients because you all mean so much to me and others, and all of the opportunity that you have given me, so I could rise to the occasion. You know who you are! Thanks so very much, you all. You are deeply admired and regarded by me as true quality. Hmmm, Oh, I would also like to thank Mark Mann for his kind heart of letting me reside at his living quarters. He is a great guy, with great staff. Thanks big guy. You are never forgotten. Ever.

Thanks! Also, I would like to thank my friend Frank McConnell who inspired me with gospel and the GOD word, which he always lives by and with! Thanks! Oh-Thanks for taking me to church those Sundays, I feel better about myself already. Thanks, buddy. I last but not least, want to give thanks to those who run the "Clinton House" in Howell, Michigan. Thanks, Lana(the Iguana) ha-ha, no seriously you are the best, lil Kimmy, Tom Keller, Frank, Judy and the whole rest of the care giving gang! Thanks- and God bless you always, and in always! That's a wrap! Take care! If I missed anyone, you know who you are and I, don't. SO LET ME KNOW! OOOO-I ALSO WANT TO THANK MY LAST GIRLFRIEND, TRACI LEE TURNER, I STILL MISS AND LOVE YOU!!!! BYE-Y'ALL!!!!

SEPTEMBER 2009
BRIAN MOILANEN

ABOUT THE BOOK

Now honestly think about it my reading friends, who out there really doesn't love reading great rhyming poems about diverse subjects such as faith, fantasy and not to mention even fiction. I know that I do and that is why I have written this here book, Intricate emotion! This is my first of several books that I will write for Authorhouse, and yes I anxiously await and look forward to each book that I write! I want to thank you so very much for purchasing this book and may it pleasure you according to the intensity of the merits of euphoria!

Much of Intricate Emotion is based on the key word, as I would call it….fidelity. To some of you, this may be a new word or a word that you are unclear of what the exact meaning actually is. I will give you a hand with the meaning.

Fidelity is the quality or state of being faithful. Now the secondary definition is as follows…..The attention to accuracy in details. There you go. That explains it! But this book also covers the huge exciting subject matter of fantasy. Sounds cools, huh? But, what exactly does it mean. I suppose If I were to ask that question to 20 people, I might just get 20 different answers. According to my reputable source being this here old dictionary, it says accordingly that fantasy is the free play of creative imagination. So, let your spirits run wild! Never….I repeat….NEVER SHOULD YOU STOP DREAMING! I hope that you enjoy the fantasy based poems in this book and I hope that they may help to positively inspire EVEN you! The last item in Intricate Emotion would have to be the section non chronologically ordered about fiction. Now, I would estimate that most of you know what fiction is. Right? If not here goes with an explanation. Fiction is, well, nothing more than something created and or made up. There you have it. I hope these poems in this here book cause you to truly think, hit an emotional tie, or maybe even possibly cause or make you think about past events or to have nostalgia. I hope to enter into your world just so you may be able to enter into mine! I hope that Intricate Emotion is breathtaking, page turning with anticipation, and even joyful as well as creates a mental journey into intricacy. Enjoy the faith, and the fantasy and not to mention the fiction . Enjoy, and may God continue to guide and bless you . Sincerely- Brian Moilanen

Index of Poems